Mud, Blood and Money

MUD, BLOOD AND MONEY

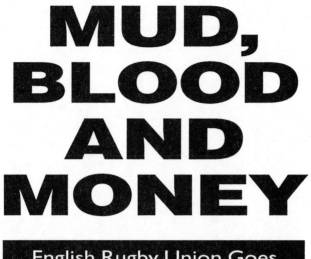

English Rugby Union Goes Professional

IAN MALIN

MAINSTREAM
PUBLISHING

EDINBURGH AND LONDON

First published in Great Britain in 1997 by
MAINSTREAM PUBLISHING COMPANY (EDINBURGH) LTD
7 Albany Street
Edinburgh EH1 3UG

ISBN 1 85158 938 4

A catalogue record for this book is available from the British Library

Typeset in Sabon
Printed and bound in Great Britain by Butler and Tanner Ltd, Frome

To Ian Tucker

Contents

The Burning of the Vanities

It was the best of times, it was the worst of times. From Thailand to Tahiti, from Moldova to Morocco, in the 1996–97 season rugby union, like a good open-side flanker, seemed to be popping up in the most unexpected places. In 1986 the sport's governing body, the International Board, had eight members. Ten years and three World Cups later, 76 countries were affiliated to the IB and all had their eyes set on the next World Cup in Wales and England in 1999. They even began playing the game in China, and with a population of 1.5 billion, and considering the size of some of those Northern Chinese, perhaps someone will one day be able to give the All Blacks a run for their money.

Rugby union, it seemed, was making claims to be a world sport. In the cradle of the game in England, though, the birth pangs of the new professional age were very painful indeed. In August 1995 the IB wrong-footed the sport's administrators by announcing that rugby union was no longer amateur. Tony Hallett, the Rugby Football Union's secretary, called the decision the 'burning of rugby's vanities'. Twickenham declared a moratorium on professionalism and set up a working-party to discuss how professionalism would work, and on 6 May 1996 the game at home officially became open. The burning of rugby's vanities then sparked a bitter squabble between England's leading clubs and Twickenham over the running of the game, and the relationship between Twickenham and its Celtic partners in the Five Nations became so combustible that England came close to being excluded from the sport's oldest competition.

In England, after months of dark days, the sport eventually reached some sunny uplands. An accord was reached and at the top Twickenham forged an alliance with its top clubs with the formation of the English Rugby Partnership, a new board comprising four representatives from the League One clubs, two from League Two, two members of the RFU and a player, the England centre and one-time theology student Damian Hopley. Hopley, appropriately, was a member of a Wasps team which would go on to win the first Courage League title of the new professional age. Tony Hallett became the board's first chief executive. The Rugby Football Union was to be run by a council, which took over from the previous unwieldy committee. This council included members of the National Clubs Association, which represented the League Three and Four clubs, and representatives of the counties and divisions. A schism in the English game was prevented but no longer was there a Courage League pyramid. It was recognised that the top two divisions were driving the game forward. Now some clubs were more equal than others.

There were many who feared the advent of professionalism and the loss of the old amateur ethos. With the players now the hirelings of their clubs, perhaps they may as well have been wearing pin-stripe suits as coloured rugby jerseys. The frequent cry was that 'It's getting to be just like soccer'. And it was true: there were the big-name foreign imports, bringing an exotic, if expensive, lustre to the Courage League and a burgeoning transfer market, there was the first big-name managerial casualty of the new era in John Hall at Bath and by the end of the season half the Courage League One clubs were in serious financial difficulties, having paid large salaries with little or no improvement on their gate revenues. But as Tony Hallett says, 'The days of shamateurism were lost in logic. We could no longer take £2 million at the gate and only pay the players expenses. The public saw through that hypocrisy.'

This book is not, you will be grateful to read, a blow-by-blow historical account of the struggle for power. Nor is it a record of what happened on the pitch during the 1996–97 season. Rather, it is a series of sketches which, I hope, paints a broader picture. And it is seen from the perspective of a journalist who has the privilege of a place in the press-box and some of the inner sanctums of the game. But however cold and dispassionate an eye the reporter casts over events, he or she is only human. Tastes and subjective feelings come into play. If a club or a person is welcoming and friendly, one is swayed by that, and the reverse is obviously just as true. In the days before professionalism, most rugby clubs were friendly institutions which treated the reporter as a guest at a large, slightly chaotic party. You were welcome but not granted many special privileges. At the bigger clubs there would be phones that worked, decent press-boxes and helpful amateur press officers to hand you reams of statistics and offer their 'spin' on events. Clubs like Wasps and Saracens were particularly good at the art of public relations. Sometimes there would even be a free pint and a sandwich.

Other clubs were not so welcoming. There are a lot of decent people at Harlequins, for example, but I always found the club a little too haughty and austere, and its inner sanctums always remained closed. The players were also cut off from the public in their private bar. But in the summer of 1996 I arrived home from holiday to the usual pile of bills and credit-card invitations, amongst which was a nice letter from Harlequins with a press pass, car-park pass and a list of fixtures. They were now called NEC Harlequins, after their recent £1.5 million investment from the Japanese electronics company. Fat chance of any sports editor calling them that, I thought, but this was real progress. Harlequins had become a professional club with a sense of public relations. When I finally went down there the atmosphere had changed. The gatemen, who once seemed to have taken lessons from their colleagues at Lord's, couldn't have been more friendly. After the game it was still impossible to find any trace of Will Carling, but there were free drinks and PR girls murmuring things like, 'Would you like to interview Keith Wood?' I found all this extremely refreshing. Harlequins now wanted to be liked and a lot of the old haughty attitudes had been lost. The club was now selling itself to the public and, in particular, younger supporters, rather than being some enclosed club for City and public-school types. Those public-school types still have the best-looking girlfriends on the rugby circuit, though. Thankfully that's one thing that hasn't changed at The Stoop.

The best of times, the worst of times. Just in case I sound too gushing about the professional age, perhaps I should get some gripes off my chest. There were many dark days in the first season of professionalism. Perhaps the worst aspect was the very nature of the talks between Twickenham and the English Professional Rugby Union Clubs organisation which represented its leading clubs. Many of the negotiators seemed to enter these talks with an attitude about as yielding as your average front row. Some of the clubs showed brazen greed and selfishness. This reached its nadir when their England players were prevented by EPRUC from attending training sessions at Bisham Abbey, with Rob Hardwick, the Coventry prop who did show up at one session, probably feeling he had entered some strange silent order. Yes, it may have been only a tactic on the part of EPRUC, and yes, the players who were already contracted to their clubs had little choice but to stay away, but it was an unedifying spectacle.

Likewise, EPRUC had prevented its players from joining divisional sides that autumn, and so we had another unedifying sight of a completely unprepared and inadequate North side being swamped by the touring All Black Barbarians on a freezing November night in Huddersfield. The All Blacks, for they were New Zealand in all but name, were insulted, and so were the very few spectators who had paid to watch a once-proud division that had defeated the All Blacks 17 years earlier.

In Wales, Scott Quinnell refused to play for his country until December, when businessman Geoff Cartwright, who runs Global Sports Ltd in Newbridge, offered the Richmond No. 8 £10,000 to end his international exile and wear boots made by the Welsh Rugby Union kit sponsor Reebok. Quinnell had a

£16,000 deal with Puma. He said that he did not want a pay cut and that other Wales players were on £30,000 deals – which may have been true, but it all seemed like too overtly commercial a way to treat the wearing of a scarlet jersey his father Derek had been so desperate to pull on. Likewise, it may be a minor irritant, but did England have to emblazon a once classically designed white shirt with the logo of a mobile phone company? And as they enter the second season of professionalism, the Nike swoosh is also to appear on those shirts. It makes commercial sense for Twickenham to enter into a record kit and merchandising franchise with Nike, but do England players have to look like Formula One cars?

There was a real problem, too, during the 1996–97 season because of a clash of interests between English clubs and the Celtic unions. This partly stemmed from the fact that the timetable for the season was worked out when people weren't talking to each other. Thus, Bristol called off their home league game against Leicester at two days' notice because Bristol had two players in an Ireland squad that weekend. Never mind all the Leicester supporters who had already bought travel tickets and match tickets. And, from a wider perspective, the diaspora of Irish players, and to a lesser extent Welsh and Scots, in England has really eroded the quality of the club scene in those exporting countries. In areas like Cornwall and Wigan, places with a real rugby culture and long-standing rugby traditions, the game is also struggling through a mixture of lack of money and inertia.

But for all the negative things, the lack of loyalty to clubs, the tackiness, the grim-faced focusing of players and coaches on their games, the professional era has helped revitalise the game in England which, it has to be said, was getting a little stagnant. Bath and Leicester's grip on the domestic honours was tending to dull the palate, excellent clubs though they are. Wasps would make the occasional impact and Harlequins their early-season break from the pack, only to falter by winter. Bath and Leicester were simply setting standards the others could not keep pace with. Now Wasps, Harlequins, Sale, Gloucester and Saracens are all matching them stride for stride. Newcastle and Richmond are also chasing the pack. The club scene has become more vibrant

13

and more glamorous and the European Cup is offering fresh challenges.

Of course, all these clubs have their millionaire backers and consortia, and for every club like Richmond there is an Orrell, a club with little money in a rugby league area. But whatever the motives of the club owners, they have still put £30 million into a game where £30 million did not exist before. When I interviewed Nigel Wray, Chris Wright and Frank Warren for this book, they all said the same thing: they wanted to improve facilities at clubs and attract families. Those clubs had taken supporters for granted, they said, and facilities at many of the leading clubs were inadequate. They were right. And if the price to pay is a bit of over-the-top marketing and naff music, then so be it.

When the Chelsea soccer club vice-chairman Matthew Harding died early in the 1996–97 season there was an outpouring of emotion, because Harding was a fan who would wear his Chelsea shirt and drink Guinness in the local before the match. He wore his heart on his sleeve, and he loved soccer. Wray, Wright, Warren, Sir John Hall and Ashley Levett take a more dispassionate view of their clubs – which is by no means a bad thing. They are benefactors rather than speculators, and the fact that they take their pleasures seriously doesn't mean we all have to.

But the bottom line, as the businessmen might say, was the rugby. Throughout the 1996–97 season, it was immeasurably better. Gone were the drab battles between packs, the games settled by penalties. Some of the rugby was intoxicating. Partly because of the new law that forces back rows to stay bound to their packs until the ball is released from scrums, the games became more expansive, with the ball in play for much longer. It was tap and run, and there were some memorable tries. It was not just a succession of try-fests, though. Two of the best games I saw that season finished Northampton 9, Bath 6 and Leicester 18, Wasps 12. There was not a try in either match but they were great spectacles, full-bloodied contests featuring brick-wall tackling. Good old-fashioned games. The honours, ultimately, went across the Channel to France. The national side, with, to paraphrase Brian Moore, a mixture of brilliance and brutality, said adieu to Parc des Princes with a Grand Slam, whilst Brive won the European Cup with some scintillating back play that made Leicester look leaden-footed at Cardiff Arms Park. But in England the fitness levels of the full-time players allowed the game to be played at a pace unrecognisable from that of 10 or 15 years ago.

But has professionalism destroyed what Mark Bailey, the former England wing and now Cambridge don, calls the 'special qualities' of an amateur game? By this he means that distinctive spirit which forges camaraderie between players from different social backgrounds, the spirit that comes from doing something for fun. When I began writing this book I read a slim volume by Gordon Allan who used to write for *The Times*. *Not All Mud and Scrums* paints a nostalgic picture of a world before Sir John Hall, EPRUC and Sky television. Allan is someone you used to bump into at places like Old Deer Park and Rectory Field. His is a tale of Hospital Cups and County Championships. The author is mostly self-deprecatory but wonderfully Pooterish at the same time. In one memorable line he writes, 'Lansdowne Road I have never experienced, although we once spent a holiday in a hotel a couple of pitches' length from it.' But Allan taps into a vein of nostalgia and presents a lost world. He realises that rugby union, like cricket, is a game dripping with memories of days when every other player was a 'legend'.

Now rugby followers on the wrong side of 40, and that just includes me, will instantly recognise the words: 'Kirkpatrick . . . to Bryan Williams . . . This is great stuff . . . Phil Bennett covering . . . chased by Alistair Scown . . . Brilliant . . . Oh, that's brilliant . . . John Williams . . . Pullin . . . John Dawes, great dummy . . . David, Tom David, the halfway line . . . Brilliant, by Quinnell . . . This Gareth Edwards . . . a dramatic start . . . What a score!' When we hear Cliff Morgan's commentary, the try is before our eyes in glorious monochrome. But will the Barbarians be lost to history with the dawning of the professional era? Will we feel the same affection for Allan's lost world in 30 years' time when we remember the Sunday afternoons at Loftus Road and Enfield? Will there be any characters in rugby, or will players become po-faced, muscular automatons with no time to share a pint in the clubhouse?

15

Allan tells the tale of Chris Ralston, the Richmond lock in a game for which he wrote a report one Wednesday afternoon. Ralston should have been at work at the time and was anxious to hide the fact from his employers. He and Allan came to an agreement that he could be mentioned in his match report but kept out of the headline and introduction to the story. Ralston played for England and the British Lions, and the story sounds bizarre now. Players were put upon at the time – and in more recent times. Tony Swift, now the chief executive at Bath, is still indignant at how the players were treated during his playing years. 'For years people lived off the players' backs,' he said to me recently. Nobody wants to return to these shamateurish, feudal days, but the game has become less of a game for the leading players and perhaps too serious at the top level. And the gradual disappearance of the Baa-Baas from the calendar is sad. It may be just the bleating of an old romantic, but I find the silencing of the lambs a great pity. Their best matches in the modern era would always be competitive and entertaining and they were played with a smile. But in the autumn of 1997 the All Blacks would not be facing them on their tour of England, and for the first time this century the Barbarians did not have an Easter tour to Wales earlier in the year. A great shame.

There is a real fear, too, in the game that professionalism will discourage the amateur volunteer who has been the sport's lifeblood: all those accountants, doctors, caterers and groundstaff who gave up their Saturday afternoons to help their local clubs. Many people have voiced their concern to me that a new generation may not give their time so willingly. For years at Bath a familiar figure helping in the car park on match-days was Alec Lewis, who played for the club and for England in the '50s. Will Jeremy Guscott be a car-park attendant 20 years from now? Probably not.

My final concern about the new era is the nature of a bruising game which is becoming more competitive now that money is at stake. Rugby union has always teetered on a dangerous, violent precipice. There are dark alleyways in matches in which players can be mugged. The game relies on decency, self-discipline and self-restraint. New fitness levels and hours of body-building in the gym allow players now to crash into each other so relentlessly that they may soon be sewing air-bags into their shirts. This has added to the gladiatorial spectacle, but that self-restraint is vital – and so is the need to preserve bruised bodies for these physical encounters. When the Lions arrived home from their summer tour to South Africa they had barely a month before the new league season began. There was a lot of burn-out on the tour and some very battered bodies by the end – and that was just the reporters.

There may have been some desperate days in the 1996–97 season but there was only one tragic one. This book is dedicated to Ian Tucker, the Australian centre, who died of head injuries the day after playing for Oxford University at Saracens in October. His death cast a long shadow over the 1996 Varsity match. I'm not often ashamed of my profession but I was angered by the way some reporters trampled over the raw feelings of some of Tucker's team-mates with constant phone calls before the Varsity match. Ian Tucker's death was caused by a freak accident, but it once more brought into focus how dangerous a collision sport can be. The 21-day rule for resting concussed players is still abused and needs to be constantly monitored. Hopefully coaches and directors of rugby will be responsible enough not to flout it, even if it means resting key players for vital games.

But whatever the demands of the professional era, rugby union players, officials and supporters remain, with only a few exceptions, a most decent bunch. If Mark Bailey was worried about the eroding of this decency, he would have been heartened had he been at that game between Northampton and Bath. It was Armistice Day, and during the minute's silence you could have heard a pin drop. The players, heads bowed in front of the Mobbs Memorial, then went about a game of frightening ferocity with not a punch thrown in anger. It was rugby and rugby culture at its best.

My thanks go to all the players and officials who gave their time, and with never a question of reward, for the writing of this book. From Jon Williams, at Christ College, Brecon, who treated me to the best school lunch I've ever had, to Mark Bailey, Brian Ashton, Phil de Glanville, Will Greenwood, Mike Harrison, Fran

Cotton and countless others. And thanks to my sympathetic sports editor Mike Averis and colleagues at *The Guardian*, Frank Keating, Robert Armstrong, Paul Rees and Paul Fitzpatrick. But most of all thanks to my wife Debbie for keeping my nose firmly on the word processor and my children for keeping out of the way when it was.

During December my son Jack went to watch his first international at Twickenham, the game between England and Argentina. It was a pretty miserable match and my own newspaper called it 'gruesome'. The abuse poured down on the players from the Barboured hordes close to the press-box, who were most certainly not in a festive mood. In the match programme Tony Hallett, that man again, wrote that Twickenham lay at the confluence of rugby opinion. It was, he said, like 'the tea houses of Pepys's London in the Age of Enlightenment'. When I got home from the game that evening I asked my son, rather nervously, what he had thought about it. 'Fantastic,' he replied. Which proves Tony Hallett's point. Everyone is born with a divine rugby ball and different views and opinions. I hope you enjoy, and perhaps even agree with, some of the opinions in this book.

Ian Malin
St Albans
May 1997

CHAPTER ONE

From Bill to Phil

The news came crackling through Radio Four at lunchtime. News of three leaders. Boris Yeltsin was to have a heart by-pass operation, Bill Clinton was about to win a second term as President of the United States. And then the really big story of the day. Said Charlotte Green, 'The new captain of the England rugby union side was announced this morning. He is Bath's Phil de Glanville . . .' This came as a bit of a shock to me. That morning, thanks to inside knowledge, careful research and an insight into the labyrinthine mind of England's coach Jack Rowell, I had written a headline in my paper *The Guardian*: 'Dallaglio the leader of leaders.' As a prediction it didn't quite come in the Nostradamus league. 'Bloody Jack Rowell,' I muttered, hoping 5 November 1996 was the sports editor's day off.

There was a corny ceremony at Twickenham to mark the coronation of the 107th England captain and the first of the professional era. Phil de Glanville had received the news on his mobile phone the previous day. He had been playing golf near Bath with his team-mates Jon Callard, Jon Sleightholme and Henry Paul. 'I received the news with a mixture of delight and trepidation,' he said. In the recent past, in the days of Billy

Beaumont, Steve Smith and John Orwin, the news that England's rugby union team had a new captain would have had to fight to make it to the back pages of daily newspapers, let alone be on the lunchtime news bulletins. But now sport was sexy it was big business, and rugby union in England was no longer a recreational pastime for the middle classes.

Will Carling had transformed the image of the England captain and in his eight-year tenure as skipper had given the nation something to crow about. England's soccer players had only partial successes – reaching semi-finals where they were always missing penalties against Germany – and the cricket team had no success at all. But on the rugby field England, once great underachievers, actually began to consistently win matches under Carling and he became the domestic game's first real star. In his prime he was up there with Botham, Faldo, Gazza and Bruno, sportsmen who became celebrities. Carling became courted by the media – but, in the end, life in the goldfish bowl proved his undoing.

His remark about '57 old farts', made, he thought, when the tape of the Channel Four crew had stopped running, and his secret trysts with the mother of the future King of England led to two tragi-comic episodes which again propelled Carling on to the front pages at a time when his game was at last stepping into the twentieth century by going professional and finding a pitch in the great market-place of sport. So it was perhaps not the best of omens when Philip Ranulph de Glanville, in a newspaper questionnaire on the day of his coronation, said that the first person he would like to invite to his birthday party was Princess Diana.

De Glanville had experienced the type of key-hole journalism that had not really been part of his life as Bath captain but permanent member of England's 'splinter group', the replacements who kick their heels on the bench. Soon after his appointment, a tabloid newspaper phoned to say that a former girlfriend was saying less than flattering things about him and would he like to comment? 'No, thanks,' said the new boy – and he battened down the hatches and prepared for life to take a few awkward turns.

'I'd seen what had happened to Will and I didn't want to go through all that,' he said at the end of an eventful six months, as he prepared to leave with the England team for Argentina. 'The captaincy is just another England job but it had become more than that for what had happened off the field. I wanted to get back to the rugby. At first I was swamped with invitations and demands for this and that, so I filtered them through to my agent James Grant, whom I'd signed with in the pre-professional days.'

De Glanville was 28 when he was made England captain. The similarities with Carling were obvious. Both were centres, both had the same marketable good looks – one of de Glanville's nicknames in the Bath dressing-room is 'Hollywood' – and they had similar middle-class upbringings at public school and Durham University. They also had attractive wives with English-rose looks, but Yolanda Keverne has no wish, like the former Mrs Carling, Julia, to be one half of rugby's first couple. A maths teacher at a school in Bath, she has resolutely refused to talk to the press about life with 'Hollywood'. 'The tabloids don't give up trying to interview her,' says de Glanville.

During the season, as captain of a side that steamrollered Scotland, Ireland and Wales to win a Triple Crown but stumbled against the New Zealand Barbarians and France, de Glanville gave a series of interviews to the rugby press but, good student of politics that he is, managed to say a lot without revealing very much at all. Polite, dignified and diplomatic, yes. Exciting, no. 'It is a goldfish bowl, yes. I've found that you have to be careful when you let your hair down and wary all the time of your behaviour in public. It's difficult for your team-mates sometimes to understand that when you slip away while they're still enjoying themselves. But in a way it's been easier to avoid the spotlight living in Bath.'

Appearances, though, can be deceptive, for Phil de Glanville is no soft centre. Another of his ironic nicknames in the Bath dressing-room is 'Hammer' – de Glanville has had his nose broken eight times at the last count. He's not afraid to throw himself about in the heavy midfield traffic, often with painful consequences. He has also had his disagreements with Jack Rowell, the perplexing, cussed England coach with whom he fell out during the 1995 World Cup when he was selected for only two full games and left out of the final third-place play-off against France. 'I should have had a chance in the French game. For Jack not to make that choice was the biggest disappointment of the lot and I told him how I felt. This was about one o'clock in the morning, so I'm not sure the timing was perfect.'

But the only hint of controversy during his first season as England captain involved not the national team but the Lions. When Fran Cotton left de Glanville out of his initial squad for the South Africa tour, the England captain hit the roof. There were sound reasons, perhaps, for not taking de Glanville to South Africa, as the Lions suddenly had a surfeit of good centres with the return from rugby league of the Welsh pair Allan Bateman and Scott Gibbs, but leading England to a Triple Crown and not making the trip was still a snub.

Ironically, perhaps, the first England captain of rugby's professional era and the face of all those Nike hoardings – 'There are two hard and fast rules. Be hard. Be Fast' – Phil de Glanville still goes out to work. Where he can fit days in between England and Bath commitments he is a marketing consultant for a Middlesex computer company. He could be a dying breed. 'You have a short shelf-life as a professional and I want to carry on working,' he says, before rushing off for an afternoon's kicking practice with his Bath team-mates.

Burglar Bill is still on the prowl. There were no £70,000 contracts for England players in his day, but he's far from bitter. In the summer of 1985 Mike Harrison was a late call-up for the England squad in the most testing tour of all – to New Zealand. The Wakefield wing, a former schoolboy sprint champion, earned his soubriquet for a pair of interception tries in each of the two Tests against the All Blacks. At Christchurch the All Blacks were in full cry and looked set for a try, when a pass bound for John Kirwan found itself intercepted by Harrison who scorched 50 yards across the turf for a debut try. A week later in Wellington and a replica try. This time Steve Pokere's pass was plucked out of the air and Harrison, deep inside his own half, raced home for another defiant score. He was a scampering

Yorkshire terrier pursued by a pack of black wolves. The name 'Burglar Bill' was given to the lean, pale-faced Barnsley bank manager, and it stuck.

Mike Harrison became a permanent fixture in the England side, or as permanent as anyone could be in those pre-Carling days. He was a right-wing with a real cutting edge and, like Phil de Glanville, he was to receive an unexpected call to lead his country. The 7 March 1987 was an infamous day in the history of the Five Nations, with a bitter game between Wales and England at the Arms Park following which Wade Dooley, Gareth Chilcott, Graham Dawe and Richard Hill were banned for the next match. Hill, the Bath scrum-half, was England captain, and the side needed a new leader for the last game of the season: the visit to Twickenham of Scotland, then on course for a Grand Slam. England also needed a leader for the tournament that was to hasten the coming of the professional era, the first World Cup, to be held that summer in Australia and New Zealand. Mike Harrison had led Yorkshire to their victory in the County Championship and the North to the Divisional Championship. But he was not captain of his club. That honour was held by the full-back Martin Shuttleworth.

The England selectors, in the midst of yet another moribund season, may have pined for the '50s, when Yorkshire fliers like Jeff Butterfield, Frank Sykes and Peter Thompson added a bit of vim and imagination to their back line. They called Mike Harrison, and Burglar Bill was the man later appointed to bring home the swag from that first World Cup. But Harrison was slower to anticipate his call to lead England than he had been to anticipate those wayward All Black passes two years earlier. 'I got a call from Geoff Cooke at home and it came completely out of the blue,' he says. He got his first big taste of the media spotlight that night. Harrison had been the subject of interviews in the rugby press since he forced his way into the England side. He was always approachable, ever modest. 'But that night,' he says, 'I appeared on BBC's *Sportsnight* and had to go into a studio in Leeds. I had to stare at this white wall while Nigel Starmer-Smith, who was in London, asked me awkward questions about the violence at the Cardiff match – what I was going to do to stop it and all that. I'll never forgive Nigel for that. I gave some diplomatic answers about putting Cardiff behind us. But it was a new sensation for me to be in the spotlight.'

Mike Harrison knows how Phil de Glanville feels. The bank manager is now a personal banker at the NatWest in the centre of Leeds. Mike Harrison is still approachable, still the same easy-going bloke and still scampering. At 41, he is also still playing rugby. He plays for Wakefield's second XV and his life is saturated by sport. When he was made England captain a decade before de Glanville, rugby union was happily amateur, stuck in a time-warp and confined to the sports pages of newspapers. England captains did not appear on the front of magazines, did not court much attention in the tabloid press, weren't plastered over giant hoardings and were certainly not mentioned in the same breath as wives of future kings of England.

But Harrison had his second taste of unwelcome publicity before the Scotland match. 'A couple of journalists from *The Sun* came to interview me at the bank where I worked in Bradford. I would always talk to anyone and they were very pleasant. Then, at the end of the interview, one of them asked me if I would mind putting on a boxing glove and posing for a photo. I refused.' Harrison could picture the headline – 'I'll be the hammer of the Scots' or suchlike – and after the battle of Cardiff he could see what kind of overheated publicity could be coming his way.

Harrison's side did hammer the Scots and, not for the last time, end their Grand Slam dreams, and he had no rivals for the World Cup captaincy. When England did go to the World Cup, where they lost ignominiously to Wales in a quarter-final in Brisbane, Harrison noticed the stark contrast between the amateur game of Britain and the commercial opportunities being flouted by the All Blacks. 'When you saw pictures of Andy Haden and the like advertising products on hoardings and on television, you knew the All Blacks were already cashing in. We received £12 a day plus a phone call home. The bank have always been good to me but some players struggled in those days. I remember the hotel we stayed at in Sydney. It was about 500 yards from the red-light area. And we stayed in Brisbane before having a four-day treat in Hamilton Island before the quarter-finals. We were reasonably well looked after but not pampered, and players then used to discipline themselves. I look at England Under-21 sides now. They go around the pitch analysing their performances after matches and they attend media-awareness courses. In my day I couldn't wait to get off the pitch and forget about my performance, and as for media awareness, I've just always spoken to anyone within reason.'

These may have been very different times, but England players had already entered a professional era in one sense. A couple of years earlier there were still players in the England team, mightily strong men like Phil Blakeway and Colin Smart, who did a minimal amount of training. 'We'll get the ball, you just use it' was their message to their backs, and this they did pretty effectively when rugby was still a set-piece game and forwards were the honest sweats at the coal-face, digging the ball out for the backs to do all the fancy stuff. But by 1987 the England squad were training as hard as professional soccer players. The previous summer each member of the squad had been given an individual coaching schedule prepared by Tom McNab, the coach to British Olympic athletes. 'From January to May in 1987 I had about two weekends at home,' said Harrison, who by then had three young children. 'We had these fitness schedules and had to keep to them. I remember going down to London for sessions and spending all day Sunday on trains getting back to Yorkshire. I'm not complaining because that's how it was at the time and I enjoyed it. It was a great honour to be England captain and just seeing my parents in the crowd for that game against Scotland made everything worth while. Yes, I suppose players were put upon at the time but we didn't see it like that. And now I was in the England team I could phone Nike, or whoever, ask for a new pair of boots and they'd send them by Red Star the next day.'

But even Harrison noticed the anomalies in training like a professional but being treated as an amateur. A car showroom in Hull offered him a car to drive with a sponsor's logo on the side. Twickenham said 'no'. And then there is the case of Burglar Bill's Bitter. Following his exploits in New Zealand, a family brewer in Wakefield, H.B. Clark, named a guest bitter after the town's most celebrated rugby player. And this strong, full-bodied brew – 'Not really a lunchtime tipple,' says Bill, as he sips a bottle of Italian beer in a Leeds restaurant – is still selling across the country. Head brewer Richard Munro says Clark's are selling around 1,700 pints a week. But since 1985 a certain personal banker has not banked a penny, though Wakefield received a donation from the brewery. 'Now, if I'd had an agent on the case I would have been a rich man by now,' laughs Mike Harrison. But, no, he's not bitter.

He still receives copies of the children's books about Burglar Bill to sign, along with countless other requests to attend rugby dinners. But Mike Harrison doesn't have time to bask in former glories. He is a member of the RFU and North committees – 'I'm a young old fart,' he says. 'In the past year there have been countless RFU meetings and they ask me to come along but I don't often have the time. They're understanding about it, though.' And there is a new generation of sporting Harrisons to administer, with his 15-year-old daughter Fiona hoping to break into the Great Britain junior athletics squad. She is already ranked the eighth best pole-vaulter in the country, and is also a formidable long-jumper and, like Dad, sprinter. Tom McNab is now coaching her. Mike's 11-year-old son Simon is also playing rugby for the Wath-upon-Dearne club, near the family home in Barnsley. 'He's a clone of me,' says a proud dad.

'I'm often asked whether I would have preferred to have played ten years later and been a Phil de Glanville. I don't think I would. I still play sport for fun but sport and work can run parallel. In my job I talk to lots of business people and many of them don't know who I am. Being a former England captain cuts no ice with them. But if they do know who I am and want to talk about rugby, that's fine, I could do that for hours. I train two nights a week with Wakefield because it helps me wind down from work. I can eat like a pig and I'm still at my best fighting weight of 12½ stone. Sport is still a release for me. I'm taking Fiona to a Barnsley AC meet this weekend but I can't bear to watch, so I'm running myself. Pathetic, isn't it? At my age.'

The old Corinthian knows he is lucky. After he had finished school, the well-known Wakefield rugby academy Queen

Elizabeth Grammar, Mike Harrison was involved in a car crash when he was aquaplaning and his head went through the windscreen. A specialist told him he would not play sport again. The accident prevented him from going to Loughborough, the country's leading sporting college, and he entered banking instead. But after three years of defying doctors' orders and playing soccer, his old rugby master Ronald Chapman introduced him to Wakefield and he knew he was at home. He still has a passion for Barnsley FC and watching them gain promotion to the Premiership at Oakwell was one of the rare times he didn't mind being a spectator, but rugby is his first love.

'Wakefield is a family club and with people like Bryan Barley I always felt at home. I was told in the early days that I wouldn't get into the England side playing for Wakefield because they were always more unfashionable than a club like Headingley. But the good thing about them is that they always brought you down to earth when you had been playing for England. You were just treated like another member of the family. People say to me that I've never changed in all the years I've been playing, and I take that as a compliment.'

And with that, Burglar Bill is off through the hordes of shoppers in the centre of Leeds. And happy to be unrecognised in the crowd.

CHAPTER TWO

The First of the Big Spenders

For the owners and chairmen of soccer clubs it is the ultimate game of Fantasy Football. To gaze down from the finest seats in the house at the team you have bought, like sheepskin-coated Caesars, must be the next best thing to scoring that winning goal at Wembley. Jack Walker, the owner of Blackburn Rovers, and Doug Ellis, the Aston Villa chairman, may be different kinds of soccer troubleshooter – Walker shuns the limelight, preferring to be seen as a shy philanthropist, while even Ellis's best friend would not describe him as modest – but both were happy to see stands named after them. Both are umbilically linked to their clubs. Both have searched for their little bit of local immortality.

And now for Fantasy Rugby. Once rugby union turned professional, a new breed appeared: the rugby club owners. Some leading clubs, notably Leicester, continued to be member clubs. Others, notably Sir John Hall's Newcastle, took on the character of the businessmen that had taken them over. Hall and the likes of Chris Wright at Wasps, Ashley Levett at Richmond and Frank Warren at Bedford were at the vanguard of endless and often acrimonious talks between the owner clubs and Twickenham during 1996. The English Professional Rugby Union Clubs organisation, EPRUC for short, represented the League One and Two clubs, and the acronym spelt trouble for Twickenham. At one stage EPRUC threatened to break away from the Rugby Football Union and organise its own competitions, doing its own deals with television. Peter Wheeler, the chief executive at Leicester, became as tough a negotiator as he was once a player. Wheeler claimed EPRUC had £30 million to spend on the future development of grounds, facilities and players, but, ultimately, EPRUC had nowhere to run to. A deal was finally struck between the leading clubs and Twickenham on the day of the England match against Scotland in February 1997, a deal whereby the clubs who had the players' contracts agreed to release the players for international duty.

The talks were often fraught, with Sir John Hall and Cliff Brittle, the dyed-in-wool chairman of the RFU's executive committee, representing the polar extremes of thinking and a permafrost developing between them. Hall personified the owner clubs at their most hard-nosed; Brittle was the traditionalist standard-bearer of what he saw as a grass-roots democracy of junior clubs. A millionaire tax exile from the Isle of Man, he was an unlikely representative of the little man. The pair once allegedly almost came to blows.

So who are the new club owners, the rugby fantasists? Are they egos that have landed or philanthropists bravely rushing in with money where others have feared to tread? Chris Wright, Nigel Wray and Frank Warren are the W-formation who, in very different ways, have helped transform Wasps, Saracens and Bedford respectively. One week in April I ruthlessly tracked them down to their executive lairs. Well, drove and caught the tube to meet them . . .

Chris Wright once began a table-tennis school in the shed of his parents' home in Lincolnshire. He then took the local team from the Third to the First Division of the Lincolnshire League. One day he went to Sudbury, a drab suburb in north-west London, and watched the local rugby team Wasps. He liked it so much, as they say, that he bought the company. Or, more precisely, he loved the club but hated their home. It was a few months after rugby union had gone professional in England or, rather, had not gone professional. Only Sir John Hall was buying in players during Twickenham's moratorium and Wasps' most-fêted player, the former England fly-half Rob Andrew, had gone to become Newcastle's most high-profile signing.

'I went to Sudbury, shook my head and said, "How can rugby union even contemplate going professional with facilities like these?"' said Wright. 'Driving home down the A40 I passed Queens Park Rangers' ground and the idea struck me. Why couldn't the two clubs share their ground?' Wright is speaking four days after one of the most talked-about English league games of the season, the controversial, edge-of-the-seat 25–25 draw between the league leaders Wasps and the champions Bath at Loftus Road. On television the highlights look gripping and to the 11,000 shirt-sleeved supporters, including Wright, it is a sun-drenched spectacle. Alex King, the new *wunderkind* of English rugby, rounds the afternoon off with a try in the final minute and Gareth Rees ensures Wasps win a point with a nerveless conversion.

The television audience receives its highlights on BBC's *Rugby Special*. It is produced by Wright's company Chrysalis, the entertainment and television production group based close to Loftus Road in west London. Wright is the company chairman who has amassed a personal fortune of some £60 million through the group. A bearded, quietly spoken man with a transatlantic luxury lifestyle, he could be Richard Branson's reticent elder brother. He is also a compulsive sports fan who owns a string of thoroughbreds and the Sheffield Sharks basketball team.

But the first love of his sporting life is Queens Park Rangers. At the age of 50, Wright bought Rangers in the early summer of 1996 after the then owner Richard Thompson relinquished control of the club which had just lost its Premiership status. Thompson turned his attention to Leeds United and Wright moved into Loftus Road. On 5 August 1996 Wasps RFC combined with Queens Park Rangers FC under the ownership of a new company: Loftus Road plc. Wasps members were offered shares at a discount and in November Loftus Road plc was floated on the Alternative Investment Market, a sort of second division of the stock market, a market for fledgling companies. Chris Wright is its non-executive chairman.

That may sound like an 'I'm not getting too involved in this' kind of title, and power at Wasps is devolved through figures like the former England captain and scrum-half Nigel Melville, now sporting a salt-and-peppery hair colour but looking as youthful as ever, and the chief executive Geoff Huckstep. But Wright is the man in charge. The Chrysalis headquarters reflect the man. There are eccentric touches, such as the Wurlitzer jukebox in the reception and the models of Laurel and Hardy in Wright's office, Joan Armatrading bursts through the speakers downstairs and, as this is also the home of Heart 106.2 Radio, there are lots of bright young things trilling away. 'Oh, sorry I missed you, what about lunch tomorrow? Fantastic . . .'

'Yeah, I don't know what half of them do,' laughs Wright. But you guess he does know. His lair is homely, a penthouse on the sixth floor, all thick carpets on which videos and CDs are strewn. Secretaries move around him discreetly. Wright sits behind a large desk and yawns a lot. The Boss. How much did the launch on the Alternative Investment Market make? 'Oh, about £10 million, but that's ancient history,' he says airily. But on sport the questioner is on safer ground and there are no yawns. 'Some time after rugby went professional, people started sniffing around the London clubs. I got a friend to produce a report for me. I was quite sceptical at first. The attendances were low, there was little infrastructure. It had become apparent, in the meantime, that soccer clubs were no longer just playthings. They had become potentially good businesses. I had always been a QPR supporter but at the time they were not for sale. Then the Thompson family moved out and I bought the club.

'After that and my trip to Sudbury I looked at a possible merger step by step, with the local authority, with the RFU, with the clubs themselves. I think it has been fantastic for Wasps because what was their alternative? They would have ended up in the Second Division. And where was the money to come from? Players were going to be paid and we had to generate it from somewhere. There was some scepticism rather than outright hostility from the more traditional members and I can appreciate their point of view. But we couldn't stand still. We had to remain as one of the big clubs and in the first season of professionalism we have put our marker down. We couldn't have done that if we had been at Sudbury.

'We can get 19,000 in Loftus Road. It's the best club rugby venue in London. Harlequins are developing The Stoop but it's costing them money, and Saracens have found their ground at Enfield is inadequate. Saracens have moved from a park pitch but they have really only stepped up from a bicycle to a moped. In the professional era you need a car. Now we're developing Loftus Road to make it more conducive to rugby. There'll be more bars and another metre at each end of the pitch. We had nearly 11,000 to watch Bath at the end of a week when 17,000 watched us at Leicester. That was fantastic. It made it all worth while for me because I must say my heart sank when I sat with about 3,000 for the Bristol match. "Was it worth it?" I asked myself.'

Wright says the only alternative was to share a venue with Watford soccer club, but that would have threatened Wasps' London identity. 'Now we have to build up a fan base and why can't it be in London? The new laws have made the game much more spectator-friendly. It's entertaining now. You just don't see many 3–3 draws any more. We are making fans. We may not have as many as Leicester or Bath but we are a young club and a British club.'

And Wasps did not rush in to buy foreign mercenaries. Va'aiga Tuigamala was on loan until after Christmas but the All Black centre, who was paid £5,000 a game before returning to Wigan and then Newcastle, was an exception. Wasps recruited astutely, with Chris Sheasby, the disaffected No. 8 from Harlequins, going on to be called up by England for their pre-Christmas internationals. Alex King was snapped up from Bristol University and the two Scottish locks Damian Cronin and Andy Reed, who provided the pack with necessary ballast, came via the French club Bourges and Bath. During the second half of the season the centre Rob Henderson came from London Irish to fill a hole left by Tuigamala, and Kenny Logan, the Scotland wing, moved from Melrose and promptly scored a league-record five tries in a game against hapless Orrell.

Wasps' young side played some effervescent rugby during the 1996–97 season and finished worthy champions. They are still the only club to have broken the league duopoly of Bath and Leicester, having also won the title in 1990. Lawrence Dallaglio, who had taken the reins when Dean Ryan decamped to Newcastle in the autumn of 1995, led the team splendidly from the front, and there was some irony in the fact that Gareth Rees, the public school master and back-packing Canadian Corinthian, should have played such a vital role in winning this first league title of the professional era. For me the highlight was in October against the European champions Toulouse in the Heineken Cup. Toulouse came to Loftus Road with the reputation for carrying the torch for the running game. The Frenchmen were thumped 77–17. On a perfect Loftus Road surface, Wasps ran in nine tries. When Wasps took the plaudits from a crowd of 6,977, the cheers were well deserved. This was as if Arsenal had beaten Juventus 7–1 across town at Highbury.

Some rugby people are a bit sniffy about Chris Wright in a 'He's not quite one of us' way. They shouldn't be. Wright cheerfully admits to not having a rugby background. He played soccer at school. 'Lincolnshire's not exactly a hotbed of rugby,' he says. And he admits to once being a member of Rosslyn Park in order to get international tickets. But he is passionate about Wasps even if he also admits to preferring a Trevor Sinclair goal to a Kenny Logan try. 'I'm really excited about Rob Henderson and Kenny Logan. They've made a big impact,' he says before nervously calculating the run-in to the end of the season. As usual, his maths are flawless.

South Africa Road and Bloemfontein Road, between which stands Loftus Road, are names resonant of a lost empire. But Wright has built his west London sporting empire on a firm base. The Sudbury-based club was never on a solid financial footing despite all its City connections. When the game went professional, it seemed darkly prescient that the main advertisement on its clubhouse stand was for Barings Bank. Until recently another stand at Sudbury was built of old bits of Anderson shelter, but Wasps were not quite prepared for the blitz of the professional age.

Yes, Loftus Road does lack some of the old ambience of Sudbury, but Wasps are quite lucky to have the man from

Chrysalis to help them in their rebirth. Chris Wright, who admits to failing a business degree at Manchester University in the '60s, had his first job as manager of a blues band called Dr Crock and the Crackpots. He went on to manage slightly more successful rock bands like Jethro Tull, Procol Harum and Ten Years After. From the fast fingers of Alvin Lee to the fast hands of Andy Gomarsall, Chris Wright seems to have a feel for an upward trend. I don't, however, recall buying any Dr Crock and the Crackpots records back in the '60s.

Nigel Wray is the executive chairman of Burford Holdings, a property investment company with a 25 per cent shareholding in the leisure group Trocadero. Trocadero entered into a joint venture with Sega, and in the autumn of 1996 Segaworld, in the heart of London's Trocadero complex, opened to great fanfares. This was Europe's most impressive virtual reality theme park. Segaworld had some early teething problems and Wray, ever candid, admitted, 'Kids think it's heaven on earth but the parents are shuffling around carrying all the coats, they're hot, they can't buy a beer and they don't want to stay long.'

In late 1995, Nigel Wray stole a march on many of the leading clubs of England by putting £2 million and offering half a million pounds worth of shares in Saracens. At the time, to a few of us in the cramped little press-room at the back of the stand at Saracens' home in the north London suburb of Southgate, Wray explained his surprising philanthropy. He was not going to be the boss, the owner, the new mogul, he said. But he said that the ethos of rugby clubs had to change to attract new customers. They were not attractive to women or families, they were not offering decent facilities or decent food and had to be more competitive, selling themselves to a wider audience. Southgate, he said, was inadequate for a top club, being little more than a playing field with a grandstand on one side. When the ball landed on the roof of that stand, we would often be treated to a shower of rust. But that was the way things were. It somehow added to the venue's charm.

Nigel Wray wants to give the customers what they want, whether they are hot, flustered parents at Segaworld or cold, hungry women spectators at Saracens. They have paid their money, argues Wray, and their needs must be catered for or they will go elsewhere. That's entertainment. The Trocadero owns the Enid Blyton company and has completed negotiations to put Noddy on American television. Saracens own the contract of Michael Lynagh, the former Australian fly-half and captain and a man who has scored more international points than anyone in the game. Lynagh's nickname is 'Noddy', and he was to pull Saracens' strings in the new professional era.

Saracens had made a considerable mark since the formation of the Courage leagues in 1987. More glamorous clubs used to come to Southgate and were often, unexpectedly, beaten. Visiting teams hated it there. The dressing-rooms were so cramped, the facilities barely adequate. The pitch was often a mud flat and when training there during the week, the players had to avoid the dog turds that had been deposited by the mutts who were taken for walks on that patch of playing field owned by Enfield Council.

Once Bath had been beaten there, thanks to the kicks of the Saracens full-back Sean Robinson. Robinson would have gone unrecognised in the streets of Enfield. On the other side, his brother Andy was a star back in Bath. That's the kind of club Saracens were. They were rather patronisingly labelled 'unfashionable', 'feisty' or 'plucky'. On one occasion a wayward kick from the Southgate pitch bounced into Chase Side and on to the luggage rack of a passing red London bus which carried on without any of the passengers noticing. That's the kind of club Saracens were. Suburban. And the world at large went about its business without lifting their heads to look out for them. Good players came and went: Dean Ryan, Jason Leonard, Ben Clarke. Saracens were a feeder club for the more ambitious teams in England where the expenses were more generous and chances of international recognition greater.

But although Saracens were strictly amateur, they were far from amateurish. They were a progressive club: they used a psychologist, Alma Thomas, to help the players win the mind games, they had astute coaches and they had links with Oxford University and the junior clubs and schools of Essex and

Hertfordshire. Saracens, though, had outgrown their home and were not attracting too many people from a huge and wealthy catchment area. Nigel Wray played rugby at school, for Old Millhillians and for Hampshire. He loved the game and lived in Totteridge. Wray could have got to Southgate in ten minutes to watch Saracens if he had a mind. But he never did.

The offices of Burford are just north of Oxford Street. Away from that road's tackiness and its smells of ersatz perfume that waft from the street stalls, Burford is in an area of pavement cafés, designer clothes shops and discreet offices. It is an area that reeks of real money. In Wray's office, at the top of the block, it is like a comfortable gentleman's club. Around the walls are prints of cricketers, the furniture and furnishings are tasteful. Wray is at home here.

His mother is in an office next door. She comes in twice a week to help with his mail for the Old Millhillians. A charming woman who talks a lot, she tells of how she and Wray's wife had organised his surprise 49th birthday bash at Mill Hill School the previous weekend. All the Old Millhillians and Saracens were there. 'Nigel's been working so hard, he doesn't know whether he's coming or going,' she says. But she doesn't approve of all his business enterprises. 'I told Nigel,' she says, 'that he shouldn't buy Nottingham Forest.' Typical of mums. You may be a 49-year-old millionaire but they still treat you as if you're 14.

Nottingham Forest, taken over a few weeks before by a consortium that included Wray, the former Tottenham Hotspur chairman Irving Scholar and the author Phil Soar, languish at the foot of the Premiership, and the evening before Wray has been up to Sale to see Saracens lose their fourth successive match and with it any chance of appearing in the lucrative European Cup. But he is far from downcast and makes a joke at his own expense. 'They call us profiteers, huh, more like lossiteers,' he laughs, before throwing himself on to a comfy armchair.

But Wray is far from casual about his investment. Indeed, he soon becomes quite apocalyptic. 'We still need to improve facilities,' he says, after I remind him of his original vision of what a rugby club should be. 'If over the next five years we don't get it right, then we won't be around. We still want that family audience but families won't come unless there are decent facilities.' During the 1996–97 season, Saracens moved to the home of Enfield soccer club, a team in the Icis League, the equivalent of a Fifth or Sixth Division. Southbury Road, next to the Great Cambridge Road, one of the main routes into London from Essex, is little more than three miles from Southgate, but it is relentlessly urban. Perhaps the least lovely of the venues in the division. Saracens do pick up supporters during their season at Enfield with crowds going from an average of 1,500 at Enfield to around 4,000. But it is not the venue that appeals, and many Saracens followers are unenthusiastic about their new home. So during the season Wray and his fellow directors look at a possible ground-share with Second Division soccer club Watford.

The crowds at Saracens have doubled and trebled for one reason. During 1996 Saracens buy more old masters than the Louvre. Not only Lynagh but Philippe Sella, the French centre who has become the most-capped international of all time, heads towards Enfield. And in December, the day the teams for the Varsity match are announced at the offices of the Bowring group in the City, Saracens push that story down the sports pages by announcing perhaps the most astonishing signing of the season. Feisty, unfashionable Saracens are to sign the most famous face in the game: François Pienaar, the man who 18 months earlier had received the World Cup from Nelson Mandela, is on his way to Southbury Road.

Before professionalism, Saracens' entire annual turnover was around £150,000 a year. Sometimes they would make a small profit. Treble that and you would have been able to pay the annual salaries of these three big names. Kyran Bracken, the England scrum-half, joined them, and, with the muscular flanker Richard Hill and the athletic No. 8 and captain Tony Diprose safely under contract, it was clear that Saracens meant big business. Saracens were not going to be spear-carriers in the unfolding new drama.

European rugby eluded them in the first season, though, thanks in no small part to something new money cannot guard against. Michael Lynagh passed his 33rd birthday during the autumn and his old bones took a bit of a battering during his first season in England. In only his second game, at Wasps, a tackle by Lawrence Dallaglio dumped Lynagh shoulder first on the hard Loftus Road turf and he was out for a month. In a game against West Hartlepool in March he suffered severe bruising to a thigh. A marked man in more ways than one. 'I know one man shouldn't make a team but we missed Michael for those matches,' said the Saracens coach Mark Evans wistfully.

Nigel Wray is disappointed at not finishing in the top four but he has long-term goals. 'The game may make a profit for investors in about five years' time,' he says. 'Saracens have a much nicer ground and we wouldn't have attracted players to Southgate. But we still lack real family facilities, crèches, that kind of thing. The Loftus Road formula is going the right way. It does make sense to share with soccer clubs. For Manchester United it doesn't matter that the ground is lying idle for a fortnight. They make money from elsewhere. Now Watford have shown an interest it makes sense to look at a stadium that could hold 20,000 people. Provided the grass will take it you need another sport, and modern pitch technology does allow two sports to be played back to back.'

Saracens failed to get planning permission for a purpose-built stadium next to Enfield soccer ground but Wray thinks the move has still been 'partially successful'. But, for him, the model is still Wasps and the relative luxury of Loftus Road. 'It may be almost blasphemy to the RFU but rugby is competing with bingo for customers nowadays. We are asking people to turn their backs on bingo halls, which are warm and welcoming, and come out on a freezing day and watch us. And rugby clubs have got to be more welcoming. Do you know, I still get people coming up to me and asking, "Will it be all right to come and watch Saracens?" After all this time, they think it is closed to everyone but members. Rugby clubs traditionally performed for their members and people were discouraged from going.

'I think Sundays are a good time to play matches because a whole lot of people in north London play on Saturdays and would like to watch the following day. French rugby is played on Sundays so I see no reason why we can't follow suit. I think the game has a huge future. Sky is using rugby to sell dishes and I don't think there is anything wrong with that. Sky has been great for the game and sport in general. I happen to think it's great that I can go home and watch the cricket from the West Indies or Manchester United play Liverpool. I have no problem with that. Perhaps the BBC was getting rugby too cheaply for all those years. And the sport has a great profile. It has gladiatorial violence, running and ball-skills. But despite its physical toughness, it has a good, clean image and girls, in particular, like it. I think it's a great game and that kids who play it are less likely to mug old ladies on the street corner.

'The whole culture of the game has changed. But it's changed for the better. The play is a lot more entertaining. It had to change to compete with the Southern Hemisphere and the game in France. And it's not getting more violent. I think it's quite ludicrous to suggest that someone is more likely to kick someone's head in because he's getting paid for it.

'Some supporters don't like what's happened at Saracens. It's true that the first team are only at Southgate to train nowadays and the club has been broken up, but we had no alternative. Things couldn't stay as they were. Once you are on the slippery slope, you slide down.'

Wray has no qualms about his major signings. 'Pienaar, Sella and Lynagh have been crucial to us. Wasps and Harlequins were always the most glamorous clubs in London and attracted players. I don't know for a fact but Kyran Bracken might not have come here if Michael Lynagh hadn't been at the club. We do play an insular game here and Lynagh, Pienaar and Sella can teach our players a lot. I don't think we've done enough to learn from the imports and we're idiots if we don't learn from them. We won't be afraid to bring in more but our preference will be to produce homegrown players. Saracens have always been regarded as a friendly club – but it was because we could be beaten. We want to win friends but win matches, too. Europe was important financially but, as the cliché goes, Rome wasn't built in a day.'

Wray is different from the other millionaire club owners in that he played rugby for years but, unlike so many old players, he is honest and unsentimental about the 'good old days'. He played full-back for Old Millhillians and turned out for Hampshire in the early '70s, until, as he puts it, 'I stopped because I was so bad that even I didn't enjoy it'. Playing has given him particular insights. 'When I was playing for Hampshire it was staggeringly amateur. Hampshire hardly had any training sessions. There was no coaching, no tactics and little in the way of co-ordinated play. And it was a different culture. You paid for playing. You paid for the jug of beer and stayed in the clubhouse. I was never one for drinking eight pints, singing "Eskimo Nell" and hanging around until midnight, though.'

Wray admits that the building of the club will be a long 'knitting-together process'. Certainly the culture shock in the cosy, Metroland world of Saracens has been great. Lynagh, Pienaar and Sella have brought a touch of the exotic to Saracens. But for every Michael Lynagh there is an Andy Lee, the fly-half he displaced. Lee is usually referred to as a bit of a journeyman, a useful enough player but not someone who will set Twickenham alight. Actually he is an excellent all-round sportsman, better than 98 per cent of the population will ever be. He has played soccer and cricket for England Schools, appearing in the same sides as Nasser Hussain and Graham Thorpe. When Saracens announced the signing of Lynagh, there was a swish press conference in central London and much popping of corks from celebratory bottles of Chardonnay. Richard Hill, who used to share a flat with Lee, announced that Lee hadn't been seen for a couple of days, and we all joked that perhaps he had thrown himself in the nearest canal.

Happily that wasn't the case, but Lee's rugby career has been put on hold with the arrival of the great Wallaby. Not a tragedy, just a reminder that while Saracens were on their great crusade, someone had to play for their second team, the Crusaders. Which prompted the thought of who was going to have the nerve to ask François Pienaar, who at the end of the season was made first-team coach, to play for the Crusaders if he ever dropped himself from the first team . . .

Frank Warren's office is next door to an indoor shopping precinct in the county town of Hertford. If it wasn't for the fact that there are so many other candidates, this could be the ugliest shopping precinct in the south of England. In the reception is sitting, or rather pacing up and down, a young man called Stephen Oates. His appointment with the boxing promoter is after mine, and we stare at each other like patients in a dentist's waiting-room while a television we are both too polite to switch off blares above our heads. Stephen refuses the coffee he is offered. Perceptive reporter that I am, I guess he is an amateur boxer trying to become a pro. He tells me he is the ABA bantamweight champion. 'And are you going to become professional?' I ask. 'Well, that depends on the money I'm offered,' he answers, looking at me as if I'm quite mad to ask such a stupid question.

From a sport where money is everything to a sport where it was once almost taboo, Frank Warren crossed the bridge between boxing and rugby union with barely a look down. In the reception room outside the office of his company Sports Network, posters advertise Warren's next big promotion, Prince Naseem versus Billy Hardy at Manchester's Nynex Arena. A few days earlier, Bedford's new chairman had watched his side silence Newcastle, the big guns of League Two, in a stirring game at Goldington Road, Bedford's oh-so-traditional home. Keen-eyed television viewers could spot adverts for the fight on the padding on the posts. Quick to take advantage of a relaxation by the International Board on the rules over advertising, Frank Warren was not missing a trick.

Bedford needed a few cobwebs to be blown away. 'It wasn't so much a sleeping giant as one in a coma,' says Frank candidly when we sit in his office. And he is disarmingly honest about his part in the waking-up process that brought Bedford to the brink of promotion to League One, with an appearance in the play-offs just a year after they finished bottom of League Two when no clubs were relegated during Twickenham's moratorium on professionalism. Bedford were a little slow to react to professionalism, and in July 1996 Warren and Bob Burrows, whom the promoter knew from Burrows' days as head of sport at ITV, had talks with the club and League One Sale, who had also not found a backer.

'I'm interested in all sports, and at the dawn of the professional era I could see the chance to get involved. Bob Burrows and I got together and we looked at Sale and Bedford. Sale were dithering, so we turned our attention to Bedford. Most of the facilities at Second Division grounds were terrible and although Sale were in the First, their stadium, if you can call it that, was pretty run-down. I had the idea of moving Sale to Manchester into the heart of rugby league country, but that didn't come off. I saw that Bedford were a similar kind of club and one where there wasn't much other top-quality sport in the surrounding area.' And so Warren's Sports Network invested around £2 million in Bedford. Paul Turner, who had impressed Warren during the talks with Sale, joined as player-coach, Geoff Cooke, the former England coach, became manager, and Burrows became chief executive. Soon there was not a cobweb to be seen.

Players came to wake up the giant from his slumbers: the Western Samoan flanker Junior Paramore, the Wales full-back Mike Rayer, the Canadian lock Norm Hadley and the veteran England prop Jeff Probyn. Later in the season they were joined by the South African flanker Rudolph Straeuli and, the most heralded and intriguing signing of all, Martin Offiah, the long-striding wing who became their man for all seasons, with a career at rugby league's London Broncos.

With Frank Warren's company owning half the club, there was a game early in the season that symbolised the new era. Bedford and Richmond had played each other many times during the century, but usually in friendly matches. At Goldington Road the tax-exiled copper dealer Ashley Levett, who had pumped some £2.5 million into Richmond, came face to face with the boxing promoter Frank Warren. Near them in the stand sat Tony Hallett, Richmond supporter and beleaguered secretary of the Rugby Football Union. Richmond's team, bulging with internationals, won 44–17.

Warren said, 'We had to drag the club into this new era. Bedford had debts, it was poorly run and had sponsorship deals that were rubbish. Club rugby is excellent value. It's not expensive. We have a core of fans but it is quite small and our job now is to market the club regionally. We had over 6,000 to watch us play Newcastle. There were only a hundred or so people from the North-east, so there is a potential audience there. But we need a bigger stadium with better facilities. People like to be pampered nowadays; they are more sophisticated. They want something to eat and drink, and merchandise. It will be a long-term haul to build up that base of fans. Our job is to sell the club to people that only go there once a season.'

Warren agrees with Nigel Wray that rugby has to compete with other sports and pastimes for its audience. 'Selling rugby is no different from selling boxing or soccer. With Naseem Hamed I started in halls of 1,000 people. Now he sells 20,000 tickets. We have to bring on a new generation of rugby followers just as boxing has, and market the game through the youngsters. To do that you need better facilities than Goldington Road can offer. Yes, it's nice and homely. But there's nothing there. It's just a pitch with a slope with a grandstand on one side. Grounds need to be upgraded. Twickenham was once a very traditional venue but it was upgraded beyond recognition and nobody complained, so why do people knock the clubs for doing the same thing? We've looked at sharing grounds with other clubs and rugby clubs may become more and more like NFL franchises. But we don't want to move out of the area. We can bring business to the area. It may sound horrible, but the club can be good for local business. When supporters come from places like Bath and Northampton, they may stay in local hotels, eat at local restaurants.'

Warren's involvement became more hands-on as the season progressed, and he eventually took over from Ian Bullerwell as chairman and by the end of the season had installed Geoff Cooke as chief executive. 'Originally I made an investment with the hope of having a little bit of fun along the way. But at the end of the day it was my money in there and I wanted a bigger say. I am aware of what's happening to the club on a day-to-day basis, though I don't spend a great deal of time there. With Geoff Cooke in there I feel very comfortable. He is one of the few people in sport who has impressed me. He makes rational decisions from the heart, not from the head.'

Warren left school at 15 and worked as a porter at London's Smithfield meat market before going into business, renting out vending machines to pubs. A friend persuaded him to invest in a fight and he became a boxing promoter almost by chance. 'I lost my money but I got bitten by the bug,' he once said. Now rugby is the bug and he is determined to make Bedford succeed. He admits he has made mistakes in business with the London Arena, part of his dream for a leisure revolution in the '80s, falling a victim of the recession. But his partnership with the American promoter Don King and his major deal with Sky television, which gave him the rights to Mike Tyson's British comeback, have made him one of the leading players in British sport.

Warren has a gruff charm and a refreshingly straightforward manner. He is one of the few people in the newly professionalised game who is not coy about the money the players earn. 'They are professional sportsmen who have given up their careers to compete in a dangerous sport. That is the nature of the beast. I wouldn't have thought any of them were on less than £1,000 a week,' he says. Again, it is rare that any of rugby's hierarchy will admit that rugby is a dangerous sport.

Warren is certainly a tough opponent despite the quiet, modest exterior. He once survived an assassin's bullet outside one of his boxing promotions in Barking and a year before had booked a seat on the Heathrow to New York Pan Am jet that exploded over Lockerbie. He did not get on board because his meeting in the United States was cancelled at the last minute. No wonder helping take on Twickenham and a few outmoded attitudes held few fears for him.

CHAPTER THREE

Our Friends in the North

Early in the 1996–97 season London's *Evening Standard* ran an interview with Andy Ripley, an England No. 8 during the '70s who was a celebrity at a time when rugby players, even international ones, could walk unrecognised down their own streets. Ripley was so famous that in the twilight of his career he appeared on TV's *Wogan* to plug his book. He also once won the BBC's Superstars competition and gave the prize money to Twickenham. 'I figured the most it would buy me was a second-hand mini,' he once told me in that typically insouciant way of his. The modern-day Corinthian was, and still is, something big in the City. Rugby union to him was an escape-valve, not a tap you could turn on to bring instant riches.

Ripley has always been loyal to one club: Rosslyn Park, in the south-west corner of London, whose home alongside the South Circular has hardly changed since Ripley's playing days. In the *Standard* article he pined for the game as it once was. 'Friendship and loyalty have been smashed,' he said. 'Rugby has lost its heroes. I want to have heroic figures out there. If they're chasing a few quid like me, I don't like it. It devalues them. It means they are marionettes, puppets manipulated by people with money.' But Ripley saved his most bitter scorn for Newcastle, the League

Two club bankrolled by the millions of Sir John Hall. 'I'm wary that the sugar-daddies have varying motives for putting money into clubs . . . I wouldn't say Sir John Hall is clueless about it, but he's obviously on some regional deification. Clubs are acquiring manufactured identities. I think Newcastle will fall apart.'

Five months later Newcastle met Leicester in what was up until then the biggest game of their season, a Pilkington Cup quarter-final at a packed Kingston Park. Newcastle lost 18–8 on a bleak day and Fleet Street's rugby correspondents, most of whom were making their first visit to the ground, were not impressed. Dean Ryan, the Newcastle captain and former England flanker, came in for some particularly scathing criticism. John Mason of *The Daily Telegraph* wrote, 'Too many of the activities of Dean Ryan were a miserable disgrace.' Bob Dwyer, the Leicester coach, had accused Ryan of 'taking cheap shots' and questioned why he was not shown at least a yellow card for foul play. Most of the national papers took their lead from Dwyer, condemning a mean-spirited, niggly match which Newcastle were treating as an acid test of their League One pretensions.

Mason, a forthright character who was to retire before the Lions' summer trip to South Africa, had been a trenchant critic of the owner clubs throughout the 1996–97 season. Not only was he unimpressed with what he saw on the field that afternoon, he was also not impressed with the press facilities on offer. He thundered, '*The Daily Telegraph* is returning Saturday's unused tea/coffee voucher. Plainly Sir John Hall's need is the greater. If they want a gentle lesson in public relations, try Leicester. They are the experts.' Ouch.

Now Ripley's tongue is rarely far from his cheek, and he did admit that if someone were to turn up at Rosslyn Park with £5 million he would not turn them away. And journalists often confuse public relations with how they were treated personally. If Newcastle did not roll out the red carpet for John Mason, well, so what? But these two criticisms illustrate that Newcastle, for all the games they were winning on the pitch, were not exactly winning hearts and minds outside the North-east. There has been a hostile reaction to Newcastle. To some they simply represent the starkest workings of market-forces in the new era. To some they represent a pick-six-numbers-and-get-rich-quick philosophy and are all that is bad in the professionalised game, a game which reached its nadir when Newcastle made Wigan rugby league club's Va'aiga Tuigamala the first £1 million rugby union player in February 1997.

That hostility from their southern critics is also partly due to the players whom Rob Andrew, the director of rugby at Newcastle, has recruited to the club. Ryan, the England lock Garath Archer, the New Zealander Richard Arnold and the fearsome Western Samoan Pat Lam are all, in rugby parlance, 'uncompromising' players. All have the body language that exudes menace on the field. This nastiness, to an extent, comes with the territory. Rob Andrew would not want to waste the John Hall millions on gentle, polite forwards, but as Newcastle laid other packs to waste during the 1996–97 season, the high – or low – point being a 156–5 defeat of Rugby during the autumn, it was as if Mike Tyson had been let loose on the bantamweight division. Being a sparring partner in the same ring as these rich new kids on the block was a painful experience.

The departure of Andrew for Newcastle during the previous autumn was also a squalid affair. Recruited by Hall on a five-year contract worth £750,000, Andrew, who five months earlier had propelled England into the World Cup semi-finals with his 'drop-goal that went around the world' against Australia, left his club Wasps under a cloud. He soon took Ryan, his half-back partner Steve Bates and the Ireland prop Nick Popplewell with him. The Wasps dressing-room and committee-room were divided when they discovered that Andrew was leaving for the North and tapping up players at Sudbury. After an acrimonious committee-room meeting, Andrew left abruptly one Thursday night in the glare of television arc-lights. The game had only gone professional two months earlier and in England the season's moratorium was supposed to prepare the ground for the new age. But Sir John Hall was not going to be part of some gentleman's agreement. The ground beneath Twickenham quaked.

Andy Gomarsall, the feisty scrum-half understudy to Bates at Wasps, appeared on BBC's *Rugby Special* after Andrew's departure. He declared that a 'cancer' had been removed from the club. It was an offensive metaphor, perhaps, but one which neatly lent a lie to all Wasps' official blandishments about 'wishing Rob Andrew well' and thanking him for his loyal service.

'All the criticism has been a positive for us. It has helped develop team spirit here. No one likes us but we don't care.' No, it's not a Millwall supporter but a smiling Steve Bates. In his smart grey suit and immaculate shirt and tie, Bates looks like the well-heeled City chartered surveyor that Andrew was before he headed north to take Hall's shilling. Bates won a solitary England cap against Romania in 1989, was an ungrumbling benchman for England for much of the early part of the decade and was Andrew's trusty half-back partner at Wasps. A public-school teacher, he seemed the epitome of the happy amateur rugby player, destined to play out his life as 'Sir' in corridors, muddy playing fields and classrooms once his playing career had wound down and the claims of the talkative Andy Gomarsall on his Wasps No. 9 shirt had been realised. In the autumn of 1995 Bates was about to take up a housemaster's job at Lord Wandsworth's College in Hampshire, a school where a promising fly-half called Jon Wilkinson was doing a passable imitation of Rob Andrew and heading for a place in the England Schools side.

'I saw a tremendous revolution was coming in the game and I was given a stark choice of whether to go with it or let things stay as they were. It was a massive move for me but the real thrill was moving into the coaching field with Dean, whom I had worked with for so long. We were already a team and the difference was that this would be our place of work each day. I'm really enjoying it. It's like being a surgeon who is at the forefront of his profession and pushing back the barriers. Psychologically and physically we are exploring new parameters all the time. We can become the best club in Europe and already we could take on Wales or Scotland and beat them.'

Bates, at 34, had given way in the Newcastle team to Gary Armstrong, the former Scotland scrum-half who is outstanding against Richmond that Easter Saturday afternoon in the meeting of the Courage League Two heavyweights at a heaving Kingston Park. Armstrong might object to his coach's assertion that Newcastle are better than Scotland and, anyway, there is a strong Celtic flavour to both sides. It could almost be Newcastle Scottish against London Welsh out there, and the theme music from *Local Hero* which blares from the Tannoy as Newcastle Falcons take the field is richly ironic given the cosmopolitan make-up of both teams.

Newcastle win the game by 37–17 in front of a full house of 6,000. The match is one of the season's landmark fixtures. Their 20–20 draw at Richmond six months earlier may have been inconclusive but Newcastle are streets better than the visitors who that weekend lead the division. Of these soon-to-be promoted sides, Newcastle look by far the best equipped for the top division. The following week it is no surprise that five of their players are chosen for the British Lions squad. Armstrong and the Irish prop Nick Popplewell could easily have made it seven on the evidence of this display. Armstrong is back to his forceful, ultra-physical self behind a dominant pack which scores all of Newcastle's four tries before the break.

After the game Andrew dutifully appears in the press-room to give his views about the game. Rob Andrew's imprint is firmly stamped across this club. It may be Sir John Hall's money that is financing Newcastle but Andrew can still deal in the hard currency where it matters, on the field. That afternoon he judges the strong wind like an old sea-dog, constantly dodging his frustrated markers with a neat side-step to hammer the ball into touch some 60 yards down the pitch, meat and drink to Doddie Weir and Garath Archer who win nearly every line-out. In the match programme there are six pictures of Andrew, and the MC at Kingston Park implores the crowd to 'really make yourselves heard for Rob Andrew' as if this were a pop concert or political rally. If Andrew were standing for election around here a month later, it would be no contest.

Andrew, still in kit and with evidence of a bruise coming up over his eye where he didn't quite elude one of those markers, answers the questions politely and intelligently. He has done this many times. He is only tetchy when he asks if there is anyone there from the Press Association, the agency having written something that had got under his skin that week. Old Golden Balls still conforms to his stereotype of 'the perfect son-in-law': well spoken, neat, friendly. I've always warmed to Andrew ever since my six-year-old son approached him rather nervously for his autograph after a Wasps game against Harlequins at Sudbury. Earlier Will Carling had signed his book in typically perfunctory fashion. But Andrew, who was kicking a ball around with his daughter, had chatted amiably to him. He has the common touch but is also a tough-minded, thick-skinned Yorkshireman who endured years of criticism but was the perfect fly-half for England's forward-dominated game of the early '90s. Andrew's Newcastle are a side in his image, tough and effective and destined to dominate the English game at the century's end. A frontiersman in Metroland, he's a 'Local Hero' all right without even knowing the words of the 'Blaydon Races'.

Kingston Park is reached by Newcastle's excellent Metro system, the London Underground in miniature but ten times more pleasurable to travel on. A trainspotter on the Metro would notice them. Hundreds and thousands of travellers are wearing replica Newcastle United shirts even though Kenny Dalglish's team have their feet up that weekend. (Unfortunately they also had their feet up when they were beaten 3–0 by Monaco to go out of the UEFA Cup in supine fashion earlier in the month, but that's another story.) Newcastle is a soccer-mad city. They go batty over Batty, but will they ever go bonkers over Bentley? During the week of the win over Richmond, Newcastle United made a confident debut as it appeared on the stock market for the first time. Shares opened at a premium when trading kicked off and the club was valued at just over £200 million. That debut made Newcastle United second in the Premiership table of floated soccer clubs behind Manchester United. The Geordies have touching faith despite, it seems, always finishing behind Manchester United.

Newcastle United and Newcastle Falcons are two members of Sir John Hall's Newcastle Sporting Club. In 1992, Hall, a former Coal Board surveyor turned property developer who built the

Metro Centre at Gateshead and transformed it into Britain's biggest shopping mall, took control of the ailing soccer club and began to construct a sporting empire, a kind of Barcelona without the sunshine. The self-styled 'capitalist with a social conscience' took over Newcastle Cobras, the ice-hockey team once known as Durham Wasps; Newcastle Eagles are the basketball club Hall took over in May 1996, and Newcastle Storm is a motor-racing team based at Leatherhead.

David Campbell was chairman of Newcastle Gosforth when rugby union turned professional in 1995. Campbell, who runs an export business on Tyneside, approached Hall to ask if Newcastle Gosforth could come under the wing of the Newcastle Sporting Club. Campbell, who had partnered Jack Rowell in the Gosforth second row during the '60s, had earlier attempted to link Gosforth with their neighbouring clubs but had not succeeded. Now the time was right and Kingston Park, to where the newly-tagged Newcastle Gosforth had moved in 1990, became the nest of the Falcons. But the North Road home of Gosforth had previously been sold to housing developers and many of the old players of Newcastle Gosforth were not needed by a club which concentrated on its first XV. From the remnants, Gosforth was reborn.

On the day Newcastle Falcons were beating Rugby 156–5, Gosforth were beating Newton Aycliffe 142–5. Gosforth had to begin again at the bottom. So the team which won the John Player Cup in 1976 and 1977 was thrown into Division Four of the Durham and Northumberland League, which was a little like throwing a lightweight in with a batch of strawweights. Gosforth have Richard Breakey, a fly-half who won a Scottish cap in the '70s, and the former England prop Colin White among their number. Both may be veterans but there are clearly a few more miles on the old clock. Gosforth play at Northumbria University, a couple of Andrew drop-goals away from Kingston Park, and have forged a link with the University, who will provide some future players and is now providing its floodlit pitch. The University plays on Wednesdays, the club on Saturdays.

'How many people watch us? Oh, about 40 or 50 and a dog,' chuckles Danie Serfontein, a former Rugby Football Union president and stalwart of Gosforth. Serfontein and his friend Doug Smith, a former Gosforth president, are among the Kingston Park crowd to watch Newcastle beat Richmond. There is no animosity between the clubs, they insist. Indeed, most Gosforth followers watch both clubs. 'North-east rugby would have died if it hadn't been for John Hall,' insists Serfontein, who says he has no qualms about Newcastle paying £1 million for Va'aiga Tuigamala. 'Gosforth were a superb team but they just didn't have the finance. What Steve Bates and Steve O'Neill are doing at Newcastle now is concentrating on developing players. The fruits of that will be seen.'

'Sir John Hall didn't just buy the club, he developed it,' Smith concurs. 'He had a plan, a strategy, from the off, and what he has done in the North is stop players going to rugby league. There was no consultation when he took over the club but you have to admire what he has done. Out there today we saw the sort of rugby we wanted to see in our playing careers. There are boys here who have given up their careers to play and good luck to them.'

Those fruits of Bates's playing development could be about to ripen. Jon Wilkinson, who would have been one of his pupils at Lord Wandsworth's College, has already been approached by Bates. Wilkinson played with calm assurance and slotted the goals that helped beat France Schools at Twickenham in March 1997. In the match programme he says he hopes to read Sport in the Community at university. He also hopes to become a professional rugby player. Newcastle may just have a job for him. Bates adds, 'We are lucky to have three universities on our doorstep and we can offer promising players bursaries. They won't be vast amounts, perhaps £5,000, but we have to look to the future. We've got some superb players here but my only regret is that they're not four or five years younger.'

Bates says that only Tuigamala has cost the club a transfer fee and rejects suggestions that money has bought success. But Newcastle's million-pound wage bill is a heavy price to pay for that success. Down in the Kingston Park clubhouse bar, though, are the players of the future, and here on a Saturday night it looks like any other rugby clubhouse bar. Around the walls are the wooden plaques which list the internationals of the club, or in this case three clubs. From Gosforth's (Tot) G.C. Robinson, who played for England in 1897, to Newcastle Falcons' R.P. Nesdale, the Kiwi hooker who plays for Ireland in 1997, continuity and a sense of history is restored. And there in the bar, under the watchful gaze of the indulgent bar staff, those young players wear funny hats and one wears his underpants, like a cartoon John Major, outside his trousers. They throw beer at one another and fall about laughing. Who says money can't buy happiness? And Andy Ripley shouldn't worry. This is just like I remember Saturday nights at Rosslyn Park.

CHAPTER FOUR

University Challenge

Doctor Mark Bailey stretches in his armchair in his room at Corpus Christi College. Outside in the November dusk, tourists and students in King's Parade scurry in and out of teashops with names like 'The Copper Kettle'. This is Cambridge, the only English city where, it seems, bicycles outnumber motor cars, a timeless world of optimistic gilded youth.

Apart from the computer on the young don's desk, it could be a scene from Frederick Raphael's *Glittering Prizes* and Bailey one of the novel's infuriatingly talented characters. A teacher of English medieval history, Mark Bailey once wrote a doctoral thesis on the importance of the rabbit to the medieval economy. This caused a certain amount of ribbing in the dressing-room at Wasps, where he played with Corinthian dash on the wing. He also found time to captain Suffolk in cricket's Minor Counties Championship in the late '80s, win three Cambridge Blues and gain seven England caps between 1984 and 1990.

But outside this cloistered world, real life intrudes. There is a bomb scare in the city centre that afternoon and the Christmas shoppers wear a resigned air. The front-page headline in the city's evening paper warns readers of the perils of life on a local estate where drug-taking among the not-so-gilded youth is rife. And the real world is interrupting the build-up to the 115th Varsity Match and university rugby in general.

Mark Bailey has for the past four years been the universities' representative on the Rugby Football Union and he is in a unique position to detect how the onset of professionalism has hit standards in university rugby and how it is changing the nature of the Varsity Match which has had a new lease of life in recent years and which fills Twickenham in that old-world time of Tuesday afternoon a fortnight before Christmas. The university championships are being sponsored by Halifax Building Society but there was evidence earlier in the season that club scouts are cherry-picking the top young players and dissuading them from going to universities. Loughborough, a traditional nursery for British rugby, lost nearly all their best players to clubs as the season began. Bailey's Cambridge were to have had the services of the full-back Jon Ufton and the No. 8 Peter Scrivener, but these two bright English stars signed contracts with their club Wasps instead. Dominic Crotty, the brilliant young Munster full-back, had to reject a place at Oxford when he was put under contract by the Irish Rugby Union.

The commercialism of the Varsity Match has already been apparent, with Oxford and Cambridge rowing with Twickenham over the spoils of an event which has been a corporate beanfeast for City institutions wining and dining clients in the run-up to Christmas. Bailey thinks that Twickenham should be concentrating less on the income it gets from one event and more on helping Oxbridge. As he says, this game is the vital lifeline for Oxbridge rugby, which, unlike the other universities, does not compete in the British Universities Sports Association Championship.

'People come up to me at the RFU and say, "Look at all these bloody foreigners in the Varsity Match," but, as I tell them, there isn't a lot we can do to keep the English players at Oxford and Cambridge,' says Bailey. 'The universities have been an important cradle for young rugby players but now those players are being drawn into the club scene.'

There were 17 Blues in the 1995 World Cup and Bailey says that Oxford and Cambridge will continue to nurture talent – but it won't necessarily be English talent. 'The universities have produced a disproportionate number of internationals over the last ten years. That may reflect the class background of the players in recent times. But the Carlings of the new world won't be playing university rugby. The contracted professionals won't be coming to universities because they will lose funding from their local education authorities. Universities may therefore have to make concessions. Harlequins and Bath, for example, have bursaries operating with their local universities.

'Oxford and Cambridge will lose an important source of international players and certain club coaches are hostile towards us. So while top-quality schoolboys are being scouted by the leading clubs, Oxford and Cambridge are attracting more attention from overseas players, particularly from the Antipodes. That's not incompatible with the roles of Oxford and Cambridge as international universities. There is a tradition of Rhodes scholars, for example. But Oxford and Cambridge will begin to benefit English rugby less and less.'

Long gone are the days where a good display in the Varsity Match could propel a chap into the Five Nations Championship the following term, but the wooden plaques on the walls of the pavilion at Grange Road which lists Blues of a light hue read like an A to Z of British rugby. Hastings, Andrew, Hall, Tony Underwood, Huw Davies, Peters, Hopley and Bailey himself are among the names from the recent past. And this month Phil de Glanville became the latest and, if Bailey is right, perhaps the last Oxford Blue to take over as England captain.

As Bailey admits, the Varsity Match continues to enjoy a remarkable popularity. 'We're delighted with that but it's difficult to explain. It's partly due to the fact that the game is one of quality and partly because of the popularity of Twickenham. But it's also the nature of the fixture, the rise of corporate hospitality and its attraction to City institutions and people within them who don't necessarily have an Oxbridge background. The Varsity Match may benefit from professionalism because in a changing world it represents a recognisable ethos and it could tap a niche in nostalgia.'

Bailey's pet theme is touched upon here. He has written an

essay on the modern game and the nature of amateurism. Professionalism, he thinks, will destroy the concept of a rugby ethos within ten or 15 years. This ethos is not amateurism but a sense of decency, comradeship and self-restraint, and a sense of proportion in what can be a dangerous, and in this Varsity Match build-up, even fatal, sport. 'There is still a cultural aversion to professionalism but pragmatism prevails now. The aversion is not anti-professional but there is a concern about the rugby spirit. It is a sociable game, socially integrated and one which all shapes and sizes can play [Neil Back may disagree with this last point] and there is a sense of self-restraint, self-discipline and nobility in the game. Restraint is important. The game is not like soccer where there are one-to-one clashes with head and feet. Here there are hidden mêlées, unseen by the eyes of officials, where the potential for serious injury lies. That's where the self-discipline is important.'

Bailey apologises for his 'pompous' essay, but it is not pompous at all. His views should be heeded, for with professionalism comes a win-at-all-costs attitude in which those mêlées could become dark alleys where the unrestrained could mug opponents. Heaven help rugby if it became a playground for the school bully.

In Bailey's day, Cambridge University could play a side like Leicester and get away with a 20-point beating by its first team. This season Cambridge play Leicester's development squad in the build-up to the Varsity Match and are hammered 87–5. It may be time to organise a fixture-list exclusively with other universities rather than the Army, RAF and Navy, fixtures resonant of a different world.

Oxford and Cambridge are both affiliated, along with 146 other British universities, to the British Universities Sports Association. 'The universities are a bastion of amateurism,' says Gethin Jenkins, a BUSA administrator. 'You don't get any money for winning our championship but there's no reason why the amateur universities and professional clubs can't co-exist. Clubs have signed our players and Alex King, for instance, is not released by Wasps to play for Brunel University. But a club like Swansea have always had an arrangement with its university to allow their student players to turn out for the college in midweek and play for the club at weekends. Durham and Bristol are trying to keep this traditional arrangement going with their local clubs. I'm optimistic that there is enough talent to go round and that professionalism won't decimate the student game.'

The worst fears of Bailey and Jenkins, though, seemed to have been realised during the week before the Varsity Match. There, in six-point type in the results section of national newspapers, was a scoreline that seemed to reflect the yawning gap between the top clubs and the unpaid students. Sale 99, Loughborough 6 was a sign of the times, it seemed. Not so, though. The Press Association had actually rung Sale's ground that night and been given the wrong scoreline by, it seems, someone who had spent the match in the club bar. The score was corrected in papers the next day to Sale 6, Loughborough 22. It just shows you can't believe what you read in the papers.

'We're trying to tack a course in an ocean where the wind is changing,' says Bailey of the universities in the brave new world of professionalism, a nice poetic touch of which Milton, an old Christ's College man, would have approved. Bailey scurries off into the evening to pick up one of his children from nursery, rather than head through The Backs to Grange Road where Cambridge that night are meeting the touring Queensland. Actually he misses an interesting game on a freezing night where the easterlies blow off the Fenlands and where the Queenslanders, jet-lagged and arriving from temperatures of 80 degrees plus, might just come unstuck.

They do. The watching Oxford players, all making notes on their opposite numbers, must have been impressed. Queensland keep their fingers warm by running in three tries in the first 17 minutes. A heavy beating looks on the cards for a Cambridge side without their captain and lock Richard Bramley. But midway through the first half the Queensland prop Matt Ryan is sent off for stamping. The tourists lose all sense of discipline and tries by the acting captain Marty Hyde and the hooker Tom Murphy along with a penalty try turn the game. Cambridge win 27–20.

Murphy is a combative character but an Australian. As if to

prove Bailey's point, not a lot of Englishmen are pressing for places in the team for the Varsity Match. But the Yorkshireman Rob Ashforth continues to prompt comparisons with Rob Andrew. The fly-half had shown great maturity a season earlier, the freshman's kicks helping to beat the touring Western Samoans. Ashforth contributes 12 points here and after the game strolls across the pitch smoking a cigarette. Doctor Bailey would probably not have approved of the cigarette but he would approve of the boy's style. And, he assures me, he isn't inhaling.

If there was ever a tragic symbol of the collision between the newly professionalised age of rugby union and the amateur world of student rugby, it was the death of Ian Tucker. There was a pall over the 1996 Varsity Match as dark and heavy as the brooding grey skies over Twickenham that day. Six weeks earlier, early on in the evening of Sunday 27 October, the life of the 23-year-old student had ebbed away in the National Hospital for Neurology and Neurosurgery in Bloomsbury.

Ian Tucker, an Australian and postgraduate social studies student at Keble College, had the previous afternoon attempted to tackle the New Zealander Henry Morgan near the end of Oxford's 33–3 defeat by Saracens at Enfield. Morgan landed on top of Tucker, who got up and carried on playing after treatment but collapsed before the final whistle and never regained consciousness. A neurosurgeon described his death from head injuries as a 'freak accident'.

And so while Ashforth and his friends were preparing for the Varsity Match with some gusto, and they would have been favourites to win anyway, Oxford were a club in mourning for much of the time leading up to what, in most of the players' cases, is the biggest match of their lives. Tucker would almost certainly have partnered Oxford's captain Quentin de Bruyn, a South African, in the centre for the match. De Bruyn, who contradicts the perceived notion that South African rugby players are not the most sensitive souls, wore his heart on his sleeve during this dark time. At the traditional City lunch hosted by Bowring, the Varsity Match sponsors, de Bruyn visibly shook with emotion as he read out the names of his side for the game the following week. There was to be no No. 12 shirt in the Oxford team in memory of Tucker, and a minute's silence was to precede the match.

The game itself was won 23–7 by Cambridge. Despite an early interception try by the Oxford centre Trevor Walsh, an Australian like Tucker, Cambridge were never really troubled and won a flat, disappointing affair via two marvellous tries by their centre Matt Singer. The game was watched by a Barboured and boozed crowd of 72,000, a record for the fixture. Gate receipts were a massive £1.6 million.

With a horrible irony, de Bruyn himself had to be replaced during the second half after suffering a bang on the head in a tackle. He was carried off the field on a stretcher, but thankfully quickly recovered from his concussion and watched the remainder of the game gloomily from the touchline. 'I had an awful feeling in the pit of my stomach and my thoughts went back to that day at Saracens,' said Oxford's director of rugby Steve Hill in an after-match press conference during which the strains of the celebrating Cambridge players singing 'Jerusalem' could be heard through the walls.

It was all too much for de Bruyn. Asked how he felt about his dead friend, the tears welled up. 'He was the fittest, most motivated guy in our side. Emotionally for myself life stopped for three days. I had virtually no sleep and found myself in a dark tunnel. It was narrow and depressing. We had lost our best player. I was out injured and he was gone and soon we lost Trevor Walsh as well. We began to play poor rugby and got into the habit of playing poorly. We did not break out of that until three weeks ago. Considering all that, the guys played their hearts out.'

De Bruyn was led away from the press conference a shattered man. He had behaved with great dignity throughout the past weeks and the journalists present were left silenced and sad. When terrible events, such as a Hillsborough or the death of a boxer, intrude on the merrily trivial world of sport, its leading players and its chroniclers sometimes don't know how to react. Here we felt we had been invited to a funeral and not known what to say to the trembly-lipped family of the deceased.

That night England A played the touring Argentinians at a

dank, cheerless Northampton. England won a no-holds-barred game, which four of their players were unable to finish, by 22–17. After an unyielding contest on an unyielding night, we found sanctuary in the warmth of the Franklins Gardens bar. A colleague ventured the opinion that, good player though he was, the England A fly-half Paul Grayson was not the type who relished the head-on tackle. Thoughts kept going back to Ian Tucker, a player whose life depended, and ended, on making that fearless front-on tackle.

CHAPTER FIVE

Union Men

The feelgood factor in the Valleys following Wales's uplifting and unexpected victory at Murrayfield at the beginning of their Five Nations campaign was soon to melt away in the chill of late January. On the field, the old Welsh virtues of darting running and fingertip passing had put the Scots to flight. Off the field, the new problems of professionalism were casting a shadow over many of Wales's leading clubs.

Llanelli, the most famous club side in the principality, were in a mess. Just before Christmas they announced that eight players newly contracted at Stradey Park had to go in an attempt to cut their wage bill by £200,000. Llanelli had negotiated some generous contracts in expectation of a £1.5 million investment from a local businessman. The money never materialised. Sugar-daddies are harder to find in West Wales than in London and Llanelli's debts were expected to reach £500,000 by the end of the season.

Llanelli, Swansea, Bridgend, Newbridge and Treorchy were eventually helped out by a £700,000 loan from the Welsh Rugby Union, following a report by the accountants Price Waterhouse into the financial state of the clubs in Wales's two top divisions. Rupert Moon, the Llanelli and former Wales scrum-half, was resigned, saying, 'If taking a pay cut means the difference between Llanelli folding or not folding, then of course I will do it.' Ironically, help was at hand from Rupert's older brother Richard, a Midlands-based employment lawyer, scrum-half of note and a founding father of the Rugby Union Players Association.

In the week following the win at Murrayfield, Richard Moon was once more leaving his solicitors' office in Leamington Spa and heading for the M5 and the long journey to Llanelli. The players' union had been officially launched in February 1996. With heavy symbolism, a Great Western train left Cardiff for Paddington, picking up supporters along the way. Since then Moon and RUPA's chairman, the former Wales and British Lions lock Bob Norster, had been busy picking up the union's new passengers, the players of England and Wales, who were paying £1 a week for their help.

Moon, an engaging 35-year-old with the Black Country twang of his native Walsall where he began and was now finishing his playing career, said, 'Between December and March Llanelli did not have a home game. This helped put the club in an even worse financial state. I was asked by the players to deal with their discussions and I met them, their chairman Stuart Gallacher and their manager Anthony Buchanan. Llanelli had to cut their wage bill by 10 per cent. Unless the money was forthcoming the club would fold. There are 26 players at Llanelli who are being paid, either as full-time or as part-time professionals. Two of them gave up jobs and their whole livelihood is tied up with the club.

'Our concern is that Llanelli are not the only club in Wales who are heading for the rocks. Professionalism could result in a massive drain of players from Wales into England. I know of one player who is playing in the second team at an English club who is earning as much as an established international in Wales. A vicious circle could form in Wales where the paying spectator won't pay to watch clubs who have been stripped of their star players, the clubs will decline and the knock-on effect will be that TV will withdraw its funding because the standard of games has dropped. The honeymoon period is over now and reality has set in. The effect is being felt in England, too. Blackheath are downsizing their squad and players from all these clubs have been ringing us to help.

'There's been a lot of discussion about who is to blame for all this. I can't put my finger on it, but I would guess that at the start of the season a whole lot of promises were made, from the governing bodies to the leading clubs and from EPRUC to the players. They haven't been able to keep those promises because there was no norm, no way of looking into the future. Many players say to me, "What am I worth?" and my stock answer is "What the market can afford". But how do you put a price on, say, Ieuan Evans, or the promising 25-year-old prop forward, or Joel Stransky?'

Moon tells two stories to illustrate the problems of professionalism in England. One was a relatively minor problem which had a happy ending. The other was more serious. 'There was a junior club in Leicestershire who had a South African playing for their third team. He was just on holiday, visiting relatives. He was not Joel Stransky, but someone playing for fun. The club wanted to register him but the RFU said he would have to serve a 60-day waiting period, by which time he would probably have been heading home. We met the registrar at Twickenham and talked the problem through. The residential time was then changed to seven days and since the start of the season the quota has changed to two foreign players per club and a seven-day waiting period.

'Then there was the case of the young player at a university in the West Midlands who rang us for help. He gave up his studies when a club promised him a career. Unfortunately things didn't work out and he was shown the door. The problem is that although rugby can be a wonderfully exciting career, young players like this are vulnerable. If I was a young player of 18 at a club like Walsall, and Bath, say, were trying to sign me, I would be flattered and maybe rush into signing. But we think players should leave their options open and think about a life after rugby.'

At least RUPA has had a painless birth, whereas professionalism itself has suffered countless pangs. The rugby unions of England and Wales welcomed union's union into the world with open arms, unlike the Football Association and the Football League 90 years earlier, when the poor trodden-on soccer stars of the day struggled to receive recognition for the PFA. The reactionaries among those running cricket at Lord's were similarly unimpressed when the England pace bowler Fred Rumsey formed the Cricketers' Association, with John Arlott as its first president, as recently as 1968. When he formed RUPA, Moon sought advice from Brendon Batson of the PFA, Nick Grimoldby, the former Sheffield Eagle who was running the rugby league players' union, and David Graveney of the Cricketers' Association.

'We want to expand the union into Scotland and Ireland, and since we began we've had calls from New Zealand and South Africa. In the Southern Hemisphere they've also discovered that there is more to the game than meets the eye. Some businessmen are driving the top clubs on but there are a huge lump of middle-ranked clubs in difficulty, while the junior clubs are not sure of where they stand in this brave new world. For these junior clubs, contracts may be the answer. Currently non-contracted players who want to move to bigger clubs can do so, but the junior club, only receives £100 when it may have invested years in that player's development. Perhaps a regulated transfer system is the answer.'

Adam Palfrey's New Year began in far from happy circumstances when the Swansea centre discovered, to paraphrase Richard Moon, that the market could no longer afford him. Swansea were once more in the vanguard in Wales during the 1996-97 season. On the pitch, that is. They were playing some wonderful attacking rugby with Scott Gibbs, having returned from his spell in rugby league with St Helens, the ringmaster in the centre at the other St Helen's. But Gibbs had returned to Swansea at a price. His six-figure salary was pushing Swansea into debt and pushing Adam Palfrey, a 25-year-old Wales A international and Cambridge Blue, on to the wing or the replacements bench.

When Palfrey was called into the office at St Helen's at New Year, he was to be told that his career at the club was at an end. Swansea, having to make cuts of around £150,000, needed to offload eight players or tear up their contracts. Palfrey, a Cardiff-based surveyor, had only arrived at Swansea from Newport six months earlier. His basic retainer, match fee and bonuses were less than £10,000, little more than he could have earned by staying at Rodney Parade. For the rest of the season he was back at Rodney Parade on a three-month contract, and he was a chastened man.

'It came as a total shock. Swansea were a great club with good coaches and it was a pleasure to play for them,' said Palfrey. 'But there were players there suffering real financial hardship. I was lucky in that I had a job. But I was considering getting a mortgage on the strength of going to Swansea. I'm relieved I didn't now. They offered to keep me on a pay-as-you-play basis, but as I'd only played six league games with Scott Gibbs now in the side, that didn't seem a very attractive proposition. When I went back to Newport I made sure I got an agent and that the contract I signed with them was more weighted in my favour than the one I had with Swansea. The whole episode taught me the value of getting proper legal advice.'

Palfrey, though, was considering a career move to an English club. His work colleague Adrian Davies had moved to Richmond the previous year and was enjoying being a full-time player at the aspiring League Two club. 'I would still like to move to England where even clubs like Bedford are offering big salaries,' said Palfrey. They were not the sentiments Richard Moon and Welsh rugby supporters necessarily wanted to hear.

Even at a financially secure club like Cardiff, the message was a gloomy one. Gareth Davies, Cardiff's chief executive and a former Wales fly-half, noted, 'We will make a loss this year from a position last year when we made £350,000. The clubs and the WRU have got to get together and sort out the future or there will be anarchy.'

Twickenham, too, was backing Richard Moon's call for some kind of regulated transfer system. Twickenham Rugby Club, that is. Twickenham are in Hertfordshire and Middlesex League Two, and although their Parkfields ground is only three miles from rugby union's HQ, it is a world away from that of Will Carling and Phil de Glanville. Founded in 1867, Twickenham is the 11th oldest club in the union, but while it may be situated down a suburban road in Hampton, Parkfields is no leafy Arcadia. Its five pitches are on land owned by Thames Water and hemmed in by a giant reservoir. The clubhouse is a concrete fortress with metal shutters to keep vandals at bay. As the players train in the semi-darkness in preparation for that weekend's vital fixture against Harrow, the word 'bleak' springs to mind.

Twickenham's players may be paid, but it is the princely sum of £20 per man for the first team if they win. Their wily treasurer made sure the annual subscription of £40 was paid by each player by withholding the first two bonuses. Twickenham play for fun, but there is a seriousness to their complaint that they nurture players from the age of seven through to Colts level and a big club like Harlequins could then sign the finished product at the age of 21 if they wished. In the days before professionalism, Twickenham would be only too glad to allow a promising young player to disappear to a first-class club. Now they are not so sure. 'If the RFU is concerned about helping the junior clubs like ours – and I think only Cliff Brittle, for all his faults, does care – then it really should look at some kind of transfer system to help us,' says Tony Kay, Twickenham's long-serving secretary, a man who played for the club in the '40s. 'Harlequins have scrapped their development squad and they will be looking to pick up players from clubs like ours. The problem is we can't very well put amateur players under contract, but we spend years teaching these youngsters, and a host of coaches and managers are putting in their time on a voluntary basis. They will continue to do so, but there has to be some return on our investment.

'Will Carling started playing at the age of seven. What will happen to the junior clubs who produce the future Will Carlings? Players will come and go to senior clubs, that's part of life, but those senior clubs have to invest in their own players. Our fly-half Danny Hudson has gone to Quins and returned here with a fairly jaundiced attitude towards them. Danny was brought up here at a club where there is an enormous body of unpaid professional work. I would hate to put a price on what one of our members, Tom Moses, and his wife do. They organise around 600 kids to play in our mini-rugby sections.'

Inside the clubhouse, the atmosphere is warm and inviting, belying the appearance of the building's outside. Twickenham RFC players were once traditionally used by England as cannon-fodder for their practice sessions. On the clubhouse walls are photographs of England's 1980 Grand Slam team pushing the junior side around. But Twickenham don't relish their role as cannon-fodder any longer. Richard Moon may find plenty of willing recruits, though, in Hertfordshire and Middlesex League Two.

CHAPTER SIX

The Image-Maker

Dick Best, the director of rugby at Harlequins, was looking at a fax on his desk that had arrived from Japan that morning. Another player was for sale and were Quins interested? 'I get one of these or a phone call every day,' he says in slightly world-weary tones. 'In a way it's good to be in the mainstream and privy to information on who's available. They come from all corners of the globe from agents or representatives of players.'

Harlequins, always the most cosmopolitan of clubs, had already signed three Frenchmen during the 1996–97 season, the forwards Laurent Benezech and Laurent Cabannes and later, to cure the perceived lack of a kicker worth his place in the side, Thierry Lacroix. Quins had been one of many clubs approached by the agent of the young Toulouse fly-half and centre Thomas Castaignède, a player famous for scoring the last-minute winning drop-goal against England in Paris in January 1996, making a childish, obscene gesture afterwards, and doing little ever since. Castaignède's agent wanted a package worth around £250,000 for his client. The France lock Olivier Roumat and the All Black flanker Michael Jones were two other players offered to Best during the season. Faxed messages asking for telephone-number salaries.

Best is ambivalent about agents just as Quins supporters have mixed feelings about many of the club's high-salary signings. From the building-site that was The Stoop arose a stadium to rank with the best in the English game, but the foundations on the pitch were still a bit wobbly. By March, Harlequins were once more out of the running for both cup and league. Despite a devastating start to the season they still managed to lose three times to unfashionable Sale, who famously trounced them in their cup semi-final at Heywood Road.

'Agents are relatively new to the game and I can see why the top players need representatives to help them explore commercial opportunities,' says Best. 'But these agents have given the players an inflated sense of their own value. More and more are getting agents – and these are not necessarily high-profile players – and ideas are put into their heads.' Best is all for the free flow of information and is one of the most approachable men on the circuit. He is happy to give the world his caustic opinions, saving his real invective for the England coach Jack Rowell, who dumped him unceremoniously after the summer tour to South Africa in 1994, when Rowell was manager and Best national coach. But Best likes to be in charge. He is a fearsome taskmaster at The Stoop and one gets the impression that agents tend to dilute the authority of figures like him in the eyes of the players. 'You're dropping me this weekend, Bestie? You'll have to see my agent about that . . .'

Agents do tend to have a bad public image, generally ranked somewhere alongside journalists and members of the Mafia, as cigar-chomping wheeler-dealers who could introduce disharmony to a meeting of the London Symphony Orchestra. The most high-profile of soccer agents is the oleaginous Eric Hall, with his puerile 'Monster, Monster' catchphrase. As the general election approached, Eric Hall urged his players to vote Tory. 'Labour wants to take my money off me. If any of my players come to me for advice I tell them to vote Tory. They've only got short careers and they have got to look after themselves.' To this voter, that sounded like a philosophy of naked greed.

There are not too many Labour Party posters on windows of the smart houses in west London's Maida Vale, where Maria

Pedro lives and from where she acts as the agent to a relatively new batch of clients, the rugby union players of the English First Division. The aforementioned Benezech and Cabannes are on her books, as is Steve Ojomoh, the Bath and former England No. 8, the Newcastle pair Tony Underwood and Nick Popplewell and, most famously, the most marketable man in the domestic game during the last decade, Jeremy Guscott. But anyone less like Eric Hall would be hard to imagine. Yes, she is smart and tough. But she is also very attractive, very pleasant and very slim with an olive skin and an intimidating c.v. Yes, a bit like old Jerry himself, the man who mysteriously made wives and girlfriends suddenly quite happy to watch 30 men wrestling in mud. Except that Jeremy Guscott has usually been above all the mud-wrestling. He's the one with the pristine white shirt bursting through the wide, open spaces with that apparently effortless acceleration, the most naturally gifted English player of his generation.

Much to Maria Pedro's delight, both Guscott and Tony Underwood were chosen for the Lions trip to South Africa. Underwood's rugby profile dipped after the 1995 World Cup in which Jonah Lomu, the enormous All Black wing, stamped over him and his reputation in that traumatic semi-final in Cape Town. But, paradoxically, Underwood became a recognisable face. He boosted his bank balance by appearing in a TV advertisement for Pizza Hut with brother Rory and Lomu. The tongue-in-cheek advert brilliantly sent up the sport and made a typically British virtue of gallant failure, a nice self-deprecatory trait so familiar to years of Wimbledon tennis watchers. Many of Tony Underwood's England team-mates, however, were unhappy at what they saw, believing the advert demeaned the side while lining the pockets of the Underwoods.

That summer England players were allowed to appear in advertisements in their England kit for the first time. This, though, hardly brought dignity to the white shirt and it was hard to imagine an All Black mocking himself in an advert after a heavy defeat. After years of fighting for their freedom to appear in advertisements, this foray into the market-place seemed to have backfired. Maria Pedro, who, she stresses, was not Underwood's agent at the time of the Pizza Hut affair, sees her role as an image-maker as much as a money-maker. When I met her over coffee at her home, it must be said that one of her clients, Nick Popplewell, had not improved his image a few days earlier when he thumped the Bedford lock Scott Murray so hard in their televised League Two game that Murray had to leave the field with bleeding behind his eye, not an action to endear yourself to potential sponsors.

Maria Pedro said, 'I'd received an offer from an advertising agency to do another TV advert featuring Tony and Lomu. I said no. He's a serious sportsman, he's good at what he does. He's not Eddie the Eagle continuing to send himself up. The Lomu affair is ancient history. You don't want to dwell on failure. I've also said no to any more link-ups with his brother Rory. The two are not Siamese twins.' Similarly, when Channel Four's *Big Breakfast*, a gaudy television show for bleary-eyed viewers, asked Jeremy Guscott to come in and do an interview on its bed with its then presenter Paula Yates, Maria Pedro said no. Guscott, she felt, did not need that sort of tacky profile. As the man says in his biography *At the Centre*, 'Up until now I have been able to resist the temptation to get up at half past six in the morning just to loll around with Paula. I am also leaving the delights of rugby club dinners until I am long retired.'

Guscott first met Maria Pedro just before the 1991 World Cup in Britain and France. At the time the England players had formed their own company, Playervision, to handle the commercial activities of the squad. The squad was also linked up to the Parallel Media Company, which signed it up with major marketing deals with companies such as Courage and Cellnet. It was a confused time when players could, strangely, earn money from 'non-rugby activities' such as speaking to a group of businessmen but not from rugby activities such as speaking to the sort of rugby club dinner that Guscott has side-stepped. The distinction between rugby-related and non-rugby-related activities, though, became very blurred.

Maria Pedro, once an assistant director of a City merchant bank, had absolutely no interest in rugby until she spotted Guscott in a televised game being watched by her ex-husband. In 1986 she had set up a management company to handle the commercial affairs of the rock singer Peter Gabriel, a friend since 1965 when the former Genesis frontman was at Charterhouse School and Maria a pupil at St Catherine's School in Guildford. She later branched into sport and began to handle the affairs of British athletes Mike Rosswess and Fiona May – athletics is her first sporting love – but her meeting with Guscott was a chance one.

Gabriel's Real World company is based in Bath. 'One day I was at a lunch and found myself sitting next to Jeremy's lawyer. Six months before I had seen Guscott on television. I used to hate rugby but he stood out as someone with obvious talent and charisma. Later that year I saw him at the Hong Kong Sevens. Back in Bath I saw a magazine called *Bath City Life* and there were some photographs of him modelling. Three or four weeks after this chance lunch meeting, I had a phone call from Jeremy when he suggested he needed an agent.'

Soon, as her old friend Peter Gabriel once sang, she was selling England by the pound. Her next client after the handsome Guscott was a less obviously marketable Bath stalwart. Gareth Chilcott, the four-square prop with the Odd Job hairstyle, is no sleek prowler of the catwalks, but Pedro was as intrigued by him as she had been by the glamorous centre. By the end of 1991 Chilcott was in pantomine and has had Christmas work ever since. 'Jeremy was attractive as a person, Coochie was a character,' she says. Other Bath players found their names in Pedro's contacts book. Jonathan Webb, the surgeon who helped England to their 1992 Grand Slam with his kicking and running skills at full-back, and Ben Clarke, the mobile back-row forward with the film-star looks, also became her clients.

'The thing about Jeremy Guscott is that he is brilliant at what he does. Without the skill you couldn't sell him as if he were a can of baked beans. Like him, most of the rugby guys are very personable and used to dealing with people. I'm helping them take advantage of commercial opportunities and negotiate their contracts. And there are two types of player: those who make their income primarily from rugby and those, like Guscott, who have a broader range of skills which need managing. The clients have to be of value and they have to have self-discipline and want to be successful at what they do.'

She talks a lot about IPR, Intellectual Property Rights. 'The amounts of money a player gets paid is not the only thing. There are two elements in signing up a player. The first concerns his right to play, the second concerns IPR, that's the right to sell his image and his name. For instance, when Newcastle signed Shearer for £15 million they then had the right to sell millions of pounds worth of shirts with Shearer's name. The nirvana for agents is to separate the amount of money a client gets paid with the IPR, because what drives the motor of Manchester United is merchandising. If you have a player who can move thousands and thousands of shirts with his name or image it seems fair that the player receives some money, whether it's Michael Jordan and his Chicago Bulls shirt or Alan Shearer and his Newcastle shirt.'

Or Jeremy Guscott and his England No. 12 shirt or Dean Richards and his Leicester G shirt. Could the name 'Deano' be the brand name of one much-loved master of the rolling maul and the use of the name be argued over in the High Court as 'Gazza' once was? 'Yes, rugby will go that way. It will be about branding. But rugby is still in the dark ages compared to soccer. I can see rugby digital TV and web-sites. I'd love to see a Jeremy Guscott web-site. It won't happen in Jeremy's day but it will further on. We have to broaden the demand, market the game and sell it.'

Maria Pedro predicts that a rugby transfer market will exist in the same way as a soccer transfer market – 'but not for five or ten years' – and that more players will move from club to club. 'I know players who are unhappy, the various reasons why they are unhappy and the clubs who want players. And it's not just about money. The value of an agent will be seen when clauses in these contracts the players have signed go wrong. And they will go wrong, as many clubs find themselves in financial trouble. I'm not sure whether these clubs can pay salaries.'

Has she encountered prejudice in a world that was once a male preserve? 'Yes, but I had the same problem when I was working in the City. But I quite like being underestimated. The hostility comes because I am good at what I do. I'm good at working with men. My sex and colour is not an issue. I'm not on any crusade. My only crusade is the amount of money I make. I'm nice enough, not unpleasant and can do business with anyone.'

Maria Pedro predicts more agents will come on the scene, not all of them as concerned about the image-making side of the job. She knows, too, that the big businessmen, the Sir John Halls and Frank Warrens, are not in rugby for fun and want a return for their investment. But she is not interested in players going through the motions. 'I'm interested in winners. That old adage about it being the taking part that matters is rubbish as far as I'm concerned. I can't stand the attitude of those Olympic athletes who come into the arena at the opening ceremony to wave to their mums and dads and then disappear without trace.'

Agents. Who needs them? Well, most people in an increasingly complex world, actually. I'll probably use one to sell and buy my next house. My own view is that agents are valuable to players in helping them seize their commercial opportunities while allowing them to concentrate on their job on the pitch. Where they can be a nuisance is when they get too deeply embroiled in the transfer market.

But agents are not new. Towards the end of the first season of professional rugby union and on the first day of the county cricket season, Denis Compton died. Compton was the first English sportsman to employ an agent and set the trend for today's sporting stars to earn their fortunes. On the 1948 England cricket tour to South Africa, Reg Heyter, then the Press Association's cricket correspondent, noticed that Compton had an extra suitcase. It was crammed full of letters, some offering lucrative contracts. One came from Brylcreem to say that as they hadn't heard from him, the company assumed their contract would continue on the same terms as before. On arriving home in London, Heyter and a partner, Bagenal Harvey, helped Compton treble his Brylcreem money to £1,000 – and so sporting agents were born. Maria Pedro is following in the same tradition as Heyter and Harvey in trying to make household names of rugby players. And anyone who can sell Gareth Chilcott must be taken seriously.

CHAPTER SEVEN

The First XV and the Last XV

There are 50 miles of winding Somerset road between the Recreation Ground in Bath and the Recreation Ground in Martock. But the West Country clubs are a world apart. In April 1997 the Rugby Football Union announced that the world's biggest sporting pyramid, the Courage League, was to be disbanded. The Allied Dunbar financial services group was to begin a three-year £12 million sponsorship package for the top two divisions, the League One clubs receiving £500,000 and the League Two clubs half that amount. Twickenham promised that money would be available for the smaller clubs, but the deal was highly symbolic. It effectively ended the principle of a seamless game and the ideal that all clubs, from the great to the humble, were in this together. Of the 1,169 clubs in the Courage League at the beginning of the 1996–97 season Bath, the most successful English club of the modern era, kicked off as cup-holders and champions. Martock had lost all 14 of their league games the previous season and are in Somerset League Three, at the base of the pyramid. There are also clubs up and down the land not in the Courage League, Sunday sides and pub sides, playing their own versions of 'coarse rugby'. But this is a tale of the haves and the have-nots. A tale of the first and last XVs . . .

There are times in the life of the rugby reporter when the job doesn't seem like work, when you stand back and say, 'Blimey, I'm getting paid for this.' Lest this sounds too smug, there are drawbacks to the job too, such as when you are hanging outside a dressing-room or in a clubhouse bar, summoning up the courage to ask some captain why his team have just lost 58–0. Or filing a match report from some freezing press-box where there is only one telephone. Or finding West Hartlepool. But there are the moments when you feel privileged. Well, smug. Such as when France were playing Wales during the 1997 Five Nations and in the press area before the game there was an eye-popping free lunch with the best food and wine Languedoc could offer, with a match to savour afterwards. Or flying off to a weekend in Dublin where the weather may be wretched but the welcome is always warm.

Going to Bath never seems like real work. For the Metropolitan reporter, a 90-minute train ride from Paddington transports you to the most beautiful city in England to watch arguably the best club side there has ever been. From 1984, when Bath won their first cup final, to 1996 when they won their fourth league and cup double, Bath have dominated the English game. That unstoppable momentum which brought a haul of silverware came through innovative, often breathtaking 15-man rugby. Perhaps I was lucky but I never saw a dull game at the Rec, and in the dying days of amateurism Bath always seemed to be breaking new ground.

Not content with dominating the domestic game in the second half of the '80s, they looked to Europe in the early '90s to expand their horizons. In 1991 Toulon, runners-up in the French championship, came to Bath to play England's champion club. There had been gales in the city that autumn and workmen were busy repairing the front of Bath's Guildhall when Toulon breezed in to dismantle Bath's façade of indestructibility, taking Bath apart brick by brick to win 26–14. But Bath had not been content to take their domestic dominance for granted. They played similar matches against Steaua Bucharest of Romania and France's Toulouse, a club who embraced Bath's philosophy of running rugby. This was five years before European Cup rugby became a reality, a time when players from Bath's rival English clubs, such as Harlequins, were still taking skiing holidays in January.

Jack Rowell had turned up from Gosforth back in 1976 to oversee the gradual transformation of an unfashionable club into world-beaters. Off the field Rowell instituted a regular training regime, and later there were revolutionary training methods. Tom Hudson and Dave Robson were the fitness and coaching gurus. Hudson, who like Robson had played rugby for the Army, had competed in the modern pentathlon at the 1956 Olympics. He joined Bath from Llanelli, where he had once worked with the legendary coach Carwyn James. At Bath University he worked on research into human performances and at the Rec the players were willing guinea pigs. They instigated winter training sessions in Lanzarote and Bath's players had a place in the sun.

And what players. A whole succession formed the bulwark that make the Recreation Ground an impregnable citadel. Strong characters such as Stuart Barnes, Nigel Redman, Jeremy Guscott, Tony Swift, John Hall and Andy Robinson, all of whom found places in the England team and whose photographs filled the wall of the clubhouse bar. When he left Bath to manage England in 1993, Rowell called them 'special men', and it was difficult to disagree.

The grandeur of the setting of Bath's ground somehow added to the swagger of the side. Most First Division clubs, such as Northampton, Gloucester, Leicester and Bristol, are in downbeat urban areas. But walk past the Abbey and the Pump Rooms and across Pulteney Bridge, which spans the Avon, down a winding staircase on the bridge and alongside a roaring weir and there it is. The Recreation Ground, the most attractive rugby theatre in England.

Leicester have been Bath's great rivals during the '90s but in the days before Bob Dwyer were often content to pound away with the big guns of their heavy pack. Bath have always been more visionary and outward-looking, and far more comfortable playing an expansive game. Bath and Leicester have been the cavaliers and roundheads of the English game.

But when real professionalism dawned, Bath, the amateurs

who had pioneered a professional approach, allowed other clubs to catch them up. In 1996–97, instead of being empowered by professionalism, Bath's power was momentarily cut off. 'We lost the plot while other clubs got their act together. Professionalism took our eye off what had made us successful in the past,' says Tony Swift, the chief executive of Bath Rugby plc, as he sips a Diet Coke at the bar of one of the city's many fashionable watering-holes.

Swift has been in his post since January 1997 after a traumatic period in the club's history. A managing partner in a firm of accountants, Swift was the club wing whose playing career had ended 18 months earlier at the age of 35 in typical fashion, in a pulsating Pilkington Cup final win over Wasps. He signed off by rounding Wasps' much-lauded three-quarter tyro Nick Greenstock and dabbing down the 391st try of his career. Now his life is another mad dash. 'I used to come here to enjoy myself. Now Bath is a 60–70-hour-a-week job,' he says.

Bath Rugby, as one wag said, sounds like something you might play in the privacy of your own tub with a ball of soap. More mundanely, it is the company formed when the multi-millionaire Andrew Brownsword ploughed £2.5 million of his considerable fortune into the club in the summer of 1996. Brownsword, a character who avoids the limelight, has made a fortune through a greetings card company, Forever Friends, which depicts cuddly characters so beloved of six-year-old girls. Brownsword's investment was a double-edged sword for Bath. The club began the season in the warm glow of yet another league and cup double. By February they were out of contention for any trophies for the first time since their glory trail began in 1984. And the club which had pioneered European rugby found themselves unceremoniously dumped out of the European Cup, in the first season English clubs had entered the competition, in a quarter-final at Cardiff. That trophy was to go to Brive, a previously unheralded French club, who crushed Leicester in a final at the Arms Park in January.

Behind the scenes, the club which once prided itself on its togetherness and was ruled from within by a cabal of players was in turmoil. With money to spend, Bath, ever the innovators, gave short-term contracts to Wigan's rugby league backs Jason Robinson and Henry Paul. With Super League now a summer sport, the rugby league players were available from September until the New Year. The pair had mixed fortunes. Paul was injured in his first game against Wasps while Robinson, brilliant broken-field runner though he was, found it difficult to bed himself in in the 15-man game. But having paid for the pair, Bath felt obliged to use them. Other backs were dropped to make way for them. Perhaps Bath should have recruited some forwards. They played brilliantly, such as in the midweek destructions of Swansea, hammered 87–15, and Bristol, who were beaten 76–7, but they could also be worryingly ordinary. By the time they lost their sixth league game in desultory fashion at Sale on 2 April, Bath had lost their league title.

John Hall had been appointed director of rugby in the summer of 1995 after his outstanding playing career as a Bath and England flanker had ended. In August 1996 he was promised a five-year contract. It never materialised. On 11 February, after Bath had been knocked out of the Pilkington Cup by Leicester, Hall was sacked. He was the first leading managerial casualty of the new era and his dismissal was more redolent of soccer's Premiership, in which sackings had become almost a weekly event in the early part of the season. Hall's dismissal came as a huge blow to a man whose father and grandfather had played for the club. He had come to personify the never-say-die spirit of Bath and as a player was supreme. But he was not the greatest man-manager, an often truculent character who could not throw off his 'Mr Grumpy' tag.

Hall claimed he had been undermined by a chief executive, Ed Goodhall, who had been appointed from the outside by the new regime. Goodhall would sit in on coaching sessions at Bath's training ground on the edge of the city at Lambridge. The players were also no longer in charge. In previous years those players would tell the committee what it was going to do. Bath were the first club, for instance, to stay in hotels the night before away matches instead of turning up at games after exhausting cross-country coach trips on the morning of games. Now every player's demand was questioned. A tray of sandwiches that was always available on away trips was cancelled. One leading player was reprimanded for smoking a cigar in the clubhouse after a match. Many of the players answered by not going to the clubhouse. The togetherness that had sustained the club throughout 13 triumphant seasons evaporated.

To players like Stuart Barnes, it was all too much. Using his regular slot in *The Daily Telegraph*, he wrote, 'Bath, of all teams, epitomised a club with soul throughout the '80s and the better part of the '90s, but, boosted by the poison chalice of millions, they stumbled into the mists of confusion.' Gareth Chilcott, another icon of the glory years, was just as sad. 'Hall was a great player but a club with so many internationals should have gone out and got a Bob Dwyer or an Ian McGeechan. It needs someone with no political baggage who could make hard decisions. Without doubt the whole family ethos at Bath has gone,' he said.

Poisoned chalice? Tony Swift prefers a more sober assessment as he sips his second Diet Coke. He wears a metaphorical suit, if not an actual one, on a sunny Saturday in April a couple of hours before Bath attempt to prevent a third defeat in the season by their old rivals from Leicester, who themselves are recovering from an unexpected midweek defeat at Gloucester. 'There are three important things we have to get back to: good team management, good players and good attitudes. We had all these things when we were successful but we've gone backwards in one or two of these aspects in recent times. There is going to be a huge investment in youth development. We will appoint a youth development officer and concentrate on scholarships and the coaching of young players.'

And later that week Bath Rugby plc take another member of staff on board. Jim Blair, the fitness coach of the Auckland Blues, is to join the club in an attempt to recall the days of Hudson and Robson. Blair joins a team of 36 full-time contracted players and 10 Academy players, three full-time coaches and two player-development officers. Swift is anxious to play down the events of the first half of the season and look to the future. His main gripe is about the Recreation Ground itself, which he describes in less glowing terms than my own. 'It's a dump,' he says matter-offactly. 'You may think it has charm, but try telling that to some of those spectators at five to three who can't see the pitch properly. It is totally inadequate for our needs.'

The leased ground's setting in the middle of the city does make the development of the Rec impossible, and Bath are looking at an industrial site on the other side of the city at West Riverside with a view to building a 20,000-capacity purpose-built stadium. 'We need this, not just for Bath Rugby, but for the city as a whole. The whole package must be right to encourage families to come to matches. For the short term, though, we're staying at the Rec, but the aim is to give supporters a clear line of sight to be able to watch the game.'

On reaching the ground just before the match, you can see why Swift is so unsentimental about the ground where he scored all those tries. And you realise why Bath spectators have the reputation for being a bit one-eyed. For there they are straining on tip-toe to get a glimpse of Bath versus Leicester, for all the changes in the new era still the great heavyweight clash of the English game. And what a game. It turns out to be one of the many compelling club matches of the season, with the astonishing result of Bath 47, Leicester 9. The Tigers have six of the Lions squad in their side. Bath have one in Jeremy Guscott, who helps run Leicester off their feet in a second half in which Bath score 34 points without reply. Bath also score six tries without reply in front of a sun-drenched crowd. 'We were outmuscled, outrun and outskilled by a better team,' concedes Leicester's coach Bob Dwyer, who also admits that the Tigers' title challenge is over. Guscott and Mike Catt help cut the Leicester defence to ribbons by throwing long passes across the field and Catt gives a masterly display of tactical kicking and attacking fly-half play, a worrying portent for the Lions selectors who have left him out of their squad for South Africa.

And watching all this, like some spectre at the feast, is Brian Ashton, who in the dark days of winter had resigned after six years of imaginative coaching at the club. Ashton had always been the lesser-sung half of a duo with Rowell, a Wise to Rowell's Morecambe, and only after the departure of Rowell did the Lancastrian achieve real recognition. It was significant that

Ireland, just a couple of weeks after Ashton resigned, appointed the 50-year-old and later rewarded him with a staggering six-year contract to take them to the World Cup of 2003. As Ireland's dreadful season began to unravel, that began to look like a life sentence. But if anyone can help the Irish rediscover the art of back play it is Ashton, and one suspects the swiftness of his appointment may have been to keep him away from Rowell and the clutches of the England management.

Ashton's departure was a great loss to Bath and an example of the ineptitude of the club's management. At the time it was reported that a rift had formed between him and Hall and the pair could not work together. Both subsequently denied a rift but Ashton said, 'Andrew Brownsword wasn't an intrusive figure at all but I wasn't part of the management. I suddenly felt like a peripheral figure, which was odd. For six years I worked as a schoolmaster and did the job as a hobby. But I felt I was more in charge then and more involved than when I gave up my teaching job and became a professional coach.'

Ashton had given up his job as a teacher at King's Bruton in the summer of 1996. Four months after his departure from Bath he still says 'we' when talking about his old charges. He and Hall have not spoken since Ashton left the club, he said, but he keeps in regular contact with many of the players. 'One of the problems of professionalism was that we suddenly had money and we thought we had to spend it,' Ashton says. 'But I don't think the experiment with Paul and Robinson was a failure. Henry Paul got injured and felt obliged to limp through games but Robinson was sensational. But bringing in players from outside changed the morale of the squad. Jon Callard, who was dropped, said he had had to wait four years in the seconds when Jon Webb was in the team but it was felt that now players from the outside weren't serving their apprenticeships. The equilibrium of the squad was upset. But if you're paying someone a hundred grand or whatever, you can't play him in the seconds. We had been a close-knit squad and the players obviously decided that it wasn't a meritocracy any more. That didn't dawn on me at the time.

'There were lots of decisions that were made that I wasn't consulted about. But things that I did complain about were sorted out once I'd left. Strange, that. I couldn't handle the people who were interfering. No, there wasn't a rift between John and me. But we were both strong characters who wouldn't back down. I said to him one day. "The trouble is, John, we both want to be in charge." He never replied.'

Ashton has no doubts that Bath's bad times are behind them. But he added, 'The chemistry used to work because everything was focused on the playing side and there were some very strong characters at the club. And because we trained at Lambridge, we only went to the club once every two weeks and weren't distracted by what was happening there. This isolation at Lambridge bound the players together. They would have died for each other. Around the country there was always a lot of unsaid jealousy. We were disliked in the same way that Manchester United are disliked. And every Saturday night we would put up a couple of metaphorical fingers to the rugby world after winning again. Players like Stuart Barnes would thrive on that.

'We always went forward every year on the playing side. We always said that if we stood still the other teams would catch us up. So the coaching had to be different every year. At the start of the season we decided to play this wide game that we had seen Wigan play against us. The midfield players Catt and Guscott would throw these 30-yard passes and the wings would be instructed to keep close to the touchlines. When I said we were going to do this at the start of the season, Jerry said it wouldn't work. They could be a bloody-minded lot, too.

'After Jack left the club in 1993 we knew we had to move the game on. We saw that in the second half against Leicester when we expanded the game width-wise and Leicester just couldn't defend against it. I felt nostalgic last Saturday watching them play like that. There's never been a more bloody-minded lot but I miss the players. Those people were part of something quite remarkable in an amateur game. No one wanted to be responsible for not winning a league title or a cup, so an irresistible momentum was built up. Sometimes what they did in training was phenomenal. Sometimes I felt like just standing back and watching.'

Ashton jokes that he could write a book on the 12 months in

which he went from Somerset schoolmaster to full-time club coach to international coach. He left the club a disillusioned man and was eventually replaced by Andy Robinson and Clive Woodward, the former Leicester and England centre. The old façade having been dismantled, Bath suggested that a new era of success can be built on the foundations of a cosmopolitan pack that includes the bull-like Argentinians Federico Mendez and German Llanes and the United States captain Dan Lyle, a former gridiron player and athletic No. 8. Perhaps it was too much to expect Bath to continue to dominate the game. As in life, sport runs in cycles. That is part of its compelling charm. Just as you thought the Tories were always going to be in charge, they tripped up over heavy feet of clay. Interestingly, Bath's fall from grace also coincided with the demise of Wigan, who had similarly dominated rugby league for a decade.

Sam Weller, in Dickens's *Pickwick Papers*, announced that Bath's famous mineral waters tasted 'like warm flat-irons'. In the first season of professionalism, Bath were given a taste of their own medicine. By the end of the season, though, the medicine seemed to be working.

Martock, in the early-evening spring sunshine, looks delightful. It has a Georgian market building, an old schoolhouse, a house called The Grange, a doctor's house and a rather grand-looking pub called The George in its main street. There is a mason in the same street who chips away at the yellowing Ham Hill stone that is quarried nearby. All Saints Church looms over the village portentously. If there were any old maids still bicycling to Communion anywhere in England, they would surely be here in Martock. In less enlightened times this rural retreat in South Somerset would probably have had its village idiot and village gossip.

But the youngsters who sit on the benches and walls look bored. The only entertainment advertised in the village is an evening of line dancing in the parish hall. Martock is not what you would call thrilling to anyone under the age of 30. If you want bright lights you have to travel to Yeovil. John Hole thought he could fill the gaps in a few social diaries, and in 1992 he formed a village rugby club. When you call John Hole at home his answer phone says cheerily, 'Hello, this is John and Elaine Hole. And Martock Rugby Club.' Because John Hole is 'Mr Martock' and his home the club office, and his wife Elaine washes all those green and black shirts. Across the land there are a lot of John Holes, somehow running rugby clubs with the help of iron constitutions and sympathetic wives.

It would be fair to say that another local pub, the Nag's Head, is also the club office. It is also the clubhouse, because Martock RFC has no clubhouse. The Recreation Ground is just that. It is a rugby pitch next to a couple of soccer pitches and a modern block of changing-rooms. This April Friday evening there is a soccer match at the Rec. South Somerset is traditionally a soccer area. Yeovil Town are running away with the Icis Premier Division and the following day strengthen their place at the top with a 4–3 win over Purfleet. Somerset's county rugby team also has a big match the following day. They are playing Cumbria in the County Championship final, where they lose 21–13. The final, which causes the cancellation of Martock's home friendly against Taunton III that day, is the talk of the Nag's Head on Friday night. Martock are a long way from having a player in the county side but John Hole would reject any notion that his side is playing coarse rugby. He is modelling the club on the village sides of Wales and wants it to have a passionate village identity. The local schools, Stanchester and Huish Episcopi, provide it with players, and, as far as Martock is concerned, the only way is up.

John Hole, at 37, works as a sports operation manager at Yeovil College – 'It means I run the PE there' – and used to be the landlord at the Nag's Head. When I meet him there for the first time he has already bought me the first pint of the evening. He is one of the few people ever to ask me to show my press card, not because he is paranoid but because he suspects the presence of a *Guardian* reporter to interview him in the Nag's Head is part of a 'wind-up' by a friend who is a bit of a practical joker. This is a natural suspicion because Martock are the kind of side whose match reports are barely given house-room in their local newspapers.

'But why Martock?' he asks me a couple of times throughout the evening. I say it's because I want to contrast them with a club like Bath at the apex of the Courage League. I don't say the chapter is called 'The First XV and the Last XV' because I think he may be offended and because John Hole is an extremely large prop forward who may thrust my notebook somewhere painful. And my intention is not to knock the Martocks of this world. Quite the reverse. Without the John Holes, the game would not exist. He has something of a rugby pedigree, having played for Bristol Colts in the late '70s. One of his team-mates then, the flanker Andy Dun, went on to win a solitary England cap. But a brief career in banking followed for Hole. There were no rugby careers in those days, and he moved to London.

'But I love this part of the world,' he says. 'Martock may be a pin-prick on the map but it's quite a big village. There are around 4,500 people living here. I was the landlord at the Nag's Head and played rugby at Crewkerne when I had the idea of forming a village side here. The idea was to keep it local but I didn't want it to be a beer side. We played for a season but struggled to find fixtures because other clubs thought we were upstarts, and it was a particular struggle to get clubs in Dorset to play us. The original plan was to play friendlies for three years or so before joining the league. But to encourage players to join us from football backgrounds we joined the league earlier. They felt they had to play in meaningful fixtures.'

Yes, money exchanges hands between the committee and the players, he admitted – the players pay £3 a game to play, with the match fees paying for the pitch, for a jug or two of beer and the cleaning of the kit. But professionalism, says Hole, has cast a shadow even here. 'There is a certain element who have come to this club expecting payment and one team in Somerset Three said this season that they are paying their players. But we can't pay players. We would kill for a sponsor. We've got our own development plan but professional players aren't on our agenda.'

Martock received £200 from Courage during the season, gratefully banked by the club treasurer Dave Rawlings, but not enough to buy half a set of shirts. 'It was difficult starting up a club from scratch. It had its attraction because there were no blazered committee men telling us what to do and how things were better in their day. But we had to find money for kit. For a club of our ilk to survive, it is the training facilities, the kit and the coaching that are important. More important than a tenner in the back pocket.'

Martock train on Tuesday and Thursday nights at the Rec. In bad weather they use indoor facilities at Stanchester School. 'We want to attract youngsters to the club and opposition teams can come to the Nag's Head after the game. We stress the social side of the club. It's important to break down barriers in the village. Yes, of course, the top players deserve to be paid, but the whole change to professionalism seems to have been done in an amateurish way. From a purely business point of view it doesn't make sense.'

John Hole actually told me a lot more that evening, but having put that notebook away and having drunk rather too many pints of the local fruity bitter at the Nag's Head, I can't remember too much. I remember thinking of those Bath players drinking their Lucozade and that in the beer-drinking stakes Martock are a long way from the bottom of the league. And I remember thinking of that old story about the Ireland lock Moss Keane and the young newspaper reporter who goes to interview him when he is picked for his first cap. 'What are you drinking?' asks Moss at their meeting in the local. Before the reporter has touched his drink, Moss has downed his pint and ordered another. Then they have another, and another, and another. The reporter forgets everything Moss has told him and has to go back to interview him the next day. I don't go back to the Nag's Head the next day. But rubbing shoulders with clubs like this is a nice antidote to the often po-faced world of professionalism. All power to 'Mr Martock's' elbow, I say.

CHAPTER EIGHT

In Search of the Next Jonathan Davies

It was a good weekend for Jonathan Davies. And Barry John. As the leading Wales clubs were kicking off their first games in the European Cup and Conference, with varying degrees of success, the pair were running out in the green and gold jerseys of Christ College, Brecon for the start of the oldest fixture in Welsh rugby.

Christ College have been meeting Monmouth School since 1879. The setting for the fixture is a world away from Sardis Road, where that afternoon, thanks to a commanding display by Wales's fly-half Neil Jenkins, Pontypridd win a laboured 28–22 victory over Benetton Treviso. That very modern fixture is Pontypridd's opening game in the European Cup. Brecon's ground is tucked into the rolling green hills of Powys. Between the pitches are rows of horse-chestnut trees, the walls of the old school are covered in red ivy, and in the pavilion by the first-team pitch, parents in waxed jackets sip tea. The evocative atmosphere stretches to the school chapel founded in 1250 by a group of Dominican friars who had settled on the site close to the River Usk. Plaques on the chapel walls commemorate the, often brief, lives of Breconians such as Rhys Price, a captain in the Welsh Regiment killed in the African War. Even more poignantly, another plaque celebrates the life of the 28-year-old Captain

Lionel Baker, 'killed by Waziri Tribesmen' in 1923. Baker sounds like the sort of adventurous chap who would have been playing in this fixture just before the Great War.

Breconians of a certain age are fond of reminding you that the three great eras in Welsh rugby in which six Triple Crowns and three Grand Slams were won were 1899–1900, 1910–11 and 1969–79. And it was Christ College who provided the national team with more players in these golden eras than any school in Wales. At the beginning of the century 'Spider' Llewellyn scored 16 tries in 20 matches, including four on his debut against England, while Teddy Morgan's try helped inflict the only defeat on the 1905 All Blacks. It was said that the quaintly named 'Boxer' Harding created the role of roving wing-forward. In the modern era Robert Ackerman became the fourth Breconian to win full honours at the age of 19, and his 22 international appearances before a career in rugby league make the centre Brecon's most-capped former pupil. He was also its fifth British Lion.

The air of serenity and politeness among the teachers and parents, meanwhile, does not extend to the players on the pitch in this ancient fixture as it kicks off beneath the pewter-grey skies of Powys. Monmouth, in chocolate jerseys, are captained by their No. 8 Andrew Williams who, in the tradition of school No. 8s, doesn't look as if he has shaved for a couple of days and looks as if he might be more at home at Sardis Road that afternoon. Williams throws his considerable weight around along with Brecon's pack leader and blind-side flanker Huw Conquer. The first half of the match is dire, with Brecon's centre and captain Roger Chillman and the Monmouth stand-off Stuart Manfred exchanging penalties. The tackling is unremitting, the referee's whistle constantly blows and the official regularly berates two stroppy packs.

At half-time Jon Williams, the master in charge of rugby at Brecon, reads the riot act to his players. Jonathan Davies is, appropriately, Brecon's fly-half, and after missing two kicks at goal in the first half, his penalty attempt from 15 yards after the break just scrapes over the crossbar. The kick seems to spur Brecon on. Young Jonathan lands another, more difficult, kick and after an hour Barry John, a full-back, joins the line as the ball is moved quickly from a line-out and bulldozes over from 30 yards out. The try is more JPR than Barry John but Brecon's supporters, swelled by a noisy contingent of the school's 70-strong rank of girl pupils, don't care. They go potty. Monmouth score a penalty try in the last move of the match but Brecon are more than satisfied with a 16–10 win.

The win buoys Brecon up for their fixture the following weekend at Llandovery. Then the whole school of 340 pupils will be bussed westwards along the A40 for the school's other major fixture. That game is the focus for an ancient rivalry between the towns as well as the schools, and the previous year's fixture was watched by over 2,000 spectators, more than the average attendance for a first-class game in Wales that day.

Jon Williams thinks these fixtures are more than a cosy tradition and are still relevant to the welfare of the game in Wales. 'There is still an anti-public-school attitude in Wales and schools like ours tend to be ostracised. I had to fight tooth and nail to get Andrew Lewis in the Wales Schools side six years ago and look what's happened to him.' What has happened is that Lewis, the Cardiff loose-head prop, has maintained Brecon's traditions by since being selected for Wales. But Williams is concerned about the progress made by recent Wales Schools players like Lewis. In 1990 Lewis was part of the Wales Schools squad which went to New Zealand and won all six of its games that August, including a match against New Zealand Schools in Wellington. More recently, in August 1994, Wales Schools were unbeaten in Australia, results Wales's senior squads could not even dream about.

Of that 1990 squad, in which Lewis and Scott Quinnell were outstanding, that pair, West Hartlepool's Mark Roderick and Huw Harries of Harlequins have carved a niche in the first-class game. Paul Armstrong, Jonathan Evans, Adam Palfrey, Paul Williams and Matthew Wintle have also made an impact with their Welsh clubs. But the majority of the squad have disappeared, to junior rugby or no rugby at all, and that, Williams says, is an indictment of the game in Wales.

'It's not as if the talent isn't here,' he says. 'The schools come in for a lot of criticism but a lot of teachers out there, and in state schools too, are still putting in a lot of time to produce these players. But where do they go? How come they're not coming through into the national side? I think the standard of coaching in the clubs is at the root of the problem. Also the standard of youth rugby in Wales is appalling. Many of those boys are ill-disciplined, and the Welsh Schools beat Wales Youth every year.'

Chris Webber, the head of PE at Christ College, agrees. Webber, a former centre at Newport and Cardiff, was on the Wales bench in 1980 and played regularly for Wales B. He has seen the game in Wales from many sides. 'We are still very parochial. Newbridge were saying that the other day they were going to play with an experimental side in the European Conference because they wanted to concentrate on their next Welsh League fixture. What sort of attitude is that? They should be taking European rugby seriously. There is no structure within the game here. The raw talent is there, though, and that is the frustrating thing.'

Webber's views are echoed by those of another teacher in Wales. Peter Manning finishes his lunch in the canteen at Ysgol Glantaf, a comprehensive school in Llandaff North in the suburbs of Cardiff. There is none of the tradition of Christ College here. Ysgol Glantaf is only 17 years old and Manning paints a grim picture of schools rugby in Wales.

'The talent is oozing out of players in the junior schools in Wales. At Under-11 level there are some incredible players. But with the death of the grammar schools and the teachers' strike in the '80s, things began to go awry. In England there are still the public schools to provide a supply of talent. Here there are now massive sixth-form colleges such as Neath Tertiary who run one side. It may be an extremely good side but then where do the boys go who can't make it to the first team there? They play other sports or no sports at all, or they drift off to clubs who don't educate them as well as they do in the schools.'

Manning says that this season Ysgol Glantaf have only four fixtures against Cardiff comprehensives and that he is now forced to take his team across the border into England for meaningful fixtures. 'But that costs money. It costs about £180 a coach trip into England and there's only so much fund-raising we can do. We recently received £500 from the WRU's Dragon's Trust but that's the first money I've had in 25 years of teaching. Money doesn't solve the problem but I met Terry Cobner, the WRU's director of rugby, and told him we had to address what was happening in the schools. Rugby is a complex game and time is needed to teach it. The demands of the national curriculum make this difficult. It's lucky we have Christ College, Monmouth and Llandovery, but all non-independent schools need help. The WRU has to look at ways of getting non-PE teachers involved in rugby again. Action has to be taken now or the game could die.' One of Manning's former charges is Huw Harries, now making great strides at scrum-half with Harlequins. 'There are plenty more where Huw came from, I'm sure,' says Harries's old teacher.

During the weekend of Christ College's win over Monmouth and as if to prove Chris Webber's point, Newbridge's experiment blows up in their faces when they lose their opening Conference game 62–38 to a far from awesome Glasgow District side. But for Webber and Williams their weekend has been a happy one. Not so for Andy Marriott, the master in charge of rugby at Monmouth. This is their fourth defeat in a far from successful start. Marriott's last two captains, Richard Parks and Gareth Curtis, are both earning money playing the game for Newport. 'For the first time, this year boys are actually considering a career playing rugby. I've mixed feelings about that,' says Marriott, a lock at Bath during the early '80s. In truth, on the evidence of their afternoon in Brecon, a job in rugby would not be a good career move for many of the boys in the chocolate jerseys, although great things are expected of the left-wing David Aston and Andrew Williams punches his weight in the Monmouth back row. But, on the day, what hope had they against a team including Jonathan Davies and Barry John?

Jonathan Davies senior had a good weekend too. That week Harlequins, of all clubs, had swaggered into Cardiff like a latter-day James Gang and beaten Wales's leading side 53–24 in the Anglo-Welsh League. It may have been virtually a second-team game, with both clubs saving their sides for their opening European fixtures at the end of the week, but Harlequins hardly had the look of a bunch of dirt-trackers. They played expansive, innovative rugby and Cardiff could not match their skills and pace. Quins had arrived the night before and stayed at a city-centre hotel. They were on a win bonus of £1,250 a player. In every aspect they looked the modern professional rugby club.

But Cardiff travelled to London four days later in a determined mood. At Loftus Road they won a thoroughly deserved 26–24 victory over Wasps, scoring three tries to nil, and it was Jonathan Davies, showing there is life in 33-year-old legs, who kicked the late, winning drop-goal, his second of the game. It was a genuine European contest and, as Davies said, 'We may not have the physical or financial strength of some English club sides. But when we put our best XV on the field we are very competitive.'

That week the sport's leading magazine in Britain, *Rugby World*, had voted Jonathan Davies No. 42 in its pantheon of all-time rugby greats. They may have quibbled in Wales at such a low billing, five places behind Will Carling, especially as three of the top five actually were Welsh. Davies, who returned to play for Cardiff earlier in the year after a spell in rugby league, is revered in Wales, and his departure to Widnes in 1988 was the most grievous defection north for the Welsh during that decade.

The fly-half berth in Wales has always had a particular mystique. In Wales any product of Max Boyce's 'fly-half factory' is expected to be top of the range. Jonathan Davies has the kind of alchemy deemed necessary to add a lustre to Wales's less than golden performances of recent years and it was no surprise when, during the week of Cardiff's win at Wasps, Gerald Davies – No. 5 in that pantheon, incidentally – used his influential column in *The Times* to push for his namesake's return to the Welsh jersey.

The incumbent at the beginning of the 1996–97 season, Neil Jenkins, is the most-capped fly-half and the leading points-scorer in Welsh history. The red-haired Jenkins is a wonderful kicker, a fearless tackler and a marvellous competitor but is unlikely ever to be mentioned in the same breath as JPR, Gerald, Barry or Jonathan. The admirable Jenkins, though, has shrugged off criticisms of his prosaic play over the years and has continued to amass the points for club and country.

Earlier in the year Wales did play a fly-half of the mercurial, side-stepping mould. Arwel Thomas, then at Bristol, looked young enough and undernourished enough to audition for the part of Oliver when he played, and played well, against England at Twickenham and against Scotland in Cardiff that February. But the following month in Dublin the sprite from Trebanos suffered at the hands, or rather the feet, of a rampant Irish pack. Early in the game Thomas took a high ball and was cruelly rucked over by the onrushing Irish forwards. It was, in the memorable words of one reporter, 'like watching a rag-doll trampled by a herd of wildebeest'.

Thomas's international career came to a shuddering halt and Jenkins returned for Wales's final Five Nations game against France in Cardiff, where his 11 points were as important as Robert Howley's glorious try in sealing a quite unexpected victory over the best team in the tournament. And so it was Jenkins again who inspired the game that sparked the 1996–97 European Cup into life. As another legendary Welsh No. 10, Cliff Morgan, might have said, 'What a pleasure it was to be at Sardis Road' the day Pontypridd beat Bath 19–6 on a foul day in the Rhondda.

Under murky skies Pontypridd found a silver lining against the club who had considered themselves European champions in all but name. The sight of Jenkins pinning the Bath pack into the corners with raking kicks warmed the cockles of the hearts of the soaked crowd shoehorned into the little ground. It was marvellous stuff. Pontypridd epitomise the Valleys clubs, passionate and aggressive. But it has a family feel, and this sense of community has persuaded Jenkins to reject countless offers from more fashionable clubs to stay in the Rhondda. That sort of loyalty also persuaded the lock Bob Penberthy to play a world-record 876 times for Ponty between 1961 and 1986, and had inspired the team to play above themselves to see their veteran prop Nigel Bezani into retirement with a cup-final win over the hot favourites Neath five months earlier.

'We haven't got a lot of money but the thing about Ponty is that they treat you with courtesy and respect,' said Jenkins. Only Cardiff, of the Welsh clubs, were to progress to the quarter-finals of the European Cup, but on successive weekends in the rolling hills of Brecon and the industrial heartlands of the Rhondda, the national sport seemed to be in decent enough health.

Jenkins, though, was to find himself on the replacements bench when Wales met Australia at the Arms Park at the beginning of December 1996. Jonathan Davies's eight-year exile was over. His recall for the game against the Wallabies helped put some £20,000 on the gate on a raw Sunday afternoon. The game was also the swan-song of Australia's peerless wing David Campese, playing his 101st and last Test. But both these modern greats were peripheral figures in a match the Wallabies, who were to be unbeaten on their tour, won 28–19.

In the welter of hype that preceded recall, Davies admitted that he was 'frightened' of the expectation that was bearing down on his shoulders. On the day he performed as well as could be expected for a 34-year-old deprived of too much possession. His kicking was flawless, with five kicks out of five bisecting the posts. But most of the time Davies had to cope with the close attentions of Mike Brial, the rugged Australian No. 8, and it was the chest-high tackling learned in Warrington and Widnes that was to serve Davies well that day.

Davies's recall was, admitted the Wales coach Kevin Bowring, a 'short-term' ploy, and there were few opportunities to show off the dummies of old, but he earned a touching tribute from Michael Lynagh, the former Australia fly-half now in the autumn of another illustrious career at Saracens. 'The game has changed dramatically and is closer to rugby league in many ways with runners popping off mini-rucks. They said it wasn't the same Jonathan Davies. Well, it's not the same game. I think it's a phenomenal comeback,' said Lynagh.

Hall of fame: Sir John Hall's millions have transformed the former Newcastle Gosforth club.

Ringing the changes: Frank Warren's investment took Bedford to the brink of a place among England's élite.

Seats in the stand wait for millionaire benefactors Sir John Hall and Ashley Levett.

Richmond's finest: Andy Moore, his club's player of the season, feels the force of a tackle from Newcastle's John Bentley.

Doubling up: Martin Offiah shared his time between Bedford and rugby league's London Broncos.

Minutes from tragedy: Ian Tucker (right) in his final fatal game for Oxford University at Saracens. (Photo © Formula One Pictures)

Hammer of the Scots: Andy Gomarsall celebrates Will Carling's final try in an England shirt in the 41–13 win over Scotland at Twickenham.

*Bath in full flow: Their greatest rivals Leicester are on the
receiving end at the Recreation Ground.*

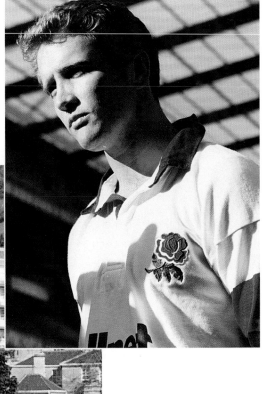
Leading man: Phil de Glanville after the announcement that he is to be the 107th England captain.

Newbury's new thoroughbreds: The Fourth Division South's champion side at their new home. (Photo © Frank Baron)

Where there's a Will: Will Greenwood, Leicester's outstanding centre, limps out of the match at Bath with an ankle injury.

Great Scott: The Richmond No. 8 Quinnell who returned to rugby union to win a place in the Lions squad.

Lion in winter: At the end of a gruelling season Leicester's Martin Johnson was chosen to lead the summer tour to South Africa.

Keeping in touch: Rob Andrew, the fly-half who recruited Newcastle's new side.

Cutting loose: Mike Catt slips his marker Walter Christofoletto as England trounce Italy.

Holding the line: Simon Shaw gets a lift in the line-out as England practise at Bisham Abbey.

Davies's return, 16 months after the game turned professional, capped an agonising time for Welsh rugby on and off the field. The drain of players to England left an obvious mark. Huw Harries was followed to Harlequins by Neath's Llewellyn brothers, the lock forwards who had just helped their club to the Heineken League title. Andrew Moore and Adrian Davies joined Richmond, who also signed the former Wales No. 8 Scott Quinnell from rugby league's Wigan and Scott's brother Craig, who followed him to the Athletic Ground. Phil Davies, Mark Ring and Kevin Moseley, players past their best but all with a lot to offer in experience and coaching skills, also left for England.

That thin top-soil of talent in Wales was to be exposed during the 1997 Five Nations Championship. Wales welcomed back the returnees from rugby league, Scott Quinnell, Allan Bateman, Scott Gibbs and David Young, for the trip to Murrayfield in January, while Arwel Thomas regained the No. 10 shirt. Wales beat the Scots in Edinburgh for the first time in 12 years, their stirring 34–19 win sealed by Thomas's interception try. So prolonged was his celebration that he almost forgot to touch the ball down in front of the dead-ball line.

This time there was no doubting Thomas, though Craig Chalmers, at fly-half for Scotland, performed fitfully before leaving the field injured three minutes from the end. 'It's nice to see there is a fly-half debate outside Wales,' said Thomas after the game, his smile as wide as Carmarthen Bay. Wales continued to play some exhilarating rugby throughout the tournament but they were careless in losing to Ireland and overpowered by the French. By the time they faced England in Cardiff, injuries had exposed that thin layer of talent and they were well beaten 34–13. Thomas was one of the injured players, enabling Jonathan Davies to play what was surely his international swan-song, although one memorable lassoing tackle on Jeremy Guscott almost helped squeeze him into the Lions squad. Fittingly, the peerless Davies kicked the last goal at the old Arms Park.

Meanwhile, Wales's leading clubs patched up their feud with their union more painlessly than England's top sides had done with Twickenham. On 21 October the WRU and the First Division clubs agreed to form an eight-strong business executive committee, comprising four members from each body. One of its first jobs was to find a sponsor for Wales's national league, the departure of Heineken having left a void in the WRU's finances. Wales can recoup some of that money once its £100 million super-stadium on the site of the Arms Park is completed in time for the 1999 World Cup. That new arena finally received Millennium money ahead of the controversial Opera House in Cardiff Bay in the summer of 1996. Now all Wales has to do is search its school playing fields to unearth a few more Jonathan Davieses to help raise the stadium's retractable roof in 1999.

CHAPTER NINE

How the West Was Lost

In the cosy clubhouse bar at Saracens' old home in Southgate, home supporters celebrated Bath's uncharacteristic beating by the then-unfashionable London club. Fortified by a pint or two, I dared suggest to Graham Dawe, the Bath hooker, that he had not been at his best that afternoon. Dawe gave me one of his narrow-eyed looks and agreed. But, he said, he had not been on top of things because at four o'clock that morning he had been giving a Caesarean section to a cow on his Cornish farm.

I had heard a lot of excuses for sporting failure in my time but this, the ultimate calf strain, was the best by a country mile. Dawe is a player of unharnessed aggression on the field, an unyielding opponent, four-square with hands like small bunches of bananas, who would have won more than his five England caps but for the presence of his old adversary Brian Moore. Off the field he is the most companionable of men. He enjoyed recalling the story of how Robert Armstrong, *The Guardian*'s rugby union correspondent, went to interview him at his farm at Milton Abbot and left rather the worse for wear after sampling farmer Dawe's home-made scrumpy. Graham Dawe is also the quintessential Cornish rugby player, the hard outdoors type in a long line of farmers, fishermen and firemen who have proudly represented the duchy. He passed his 37th birthday when the first professional season began and was still holding down a place in the Bath first team, but only just. In a match at Northampton in November he left the field in agony with a dislocated elbow. That's it for 'Dawesey', we sagely agreed. But he was back on the England bench within a month. You could not put him down.

A year after that defeat at Saracens, Dawe was a member of a Cornish side that beat Yorkshire in the most memorable of finals in County Championship history. Cornwall won the 1991 final at Twickenham 29–20 after extra-time against a side that included players as illustrious as the former England captain Mike Harrison. Cornwall, 13 points adrift at the start of the final quarter, dared not lose. Among the capacity crowd of 56,000 were an estimated 40,000 Cornish supporters, although it seemed like there were a great deal more. Bedecked in gold and black, Trelawny's army made Paddington Station at midday look like Molineux at three o'clock. The drama of that day was unbelievable.

Cornwall is a county that relishes its myths and legends, and the disused castle-like ruins of stacks and engine-houses that litter the rugged landscape are reminders of a lost Avalon. They are also reminders of the constant battle the county's tin-miners had against water. Rugby union has given Cornwall a sporting identity over the years. In 1991 those Cornish followers who believe the world stops at Plymouth were once more given a taste of what it was like when the duchy was grand and could take on the best that England had to offer.

Surprisingly, perhaps, it was only the second time Cornwall, for all its enthusiasm for county rugby, had won the County Championship. The county's high-water mark had been 1908. In those days Cornwall could not only take on England, they could take on the world. In 1908 Cornwall, representing Great Britain, won a silver medal at the Olympic Games at White City. In the final they were beaten 32–3 by Australia.

But if that was a disappointing result, 90 years on, Cornwall are hardly in a state to take on the Wallabies. Early this season on back-to-back weekends came two other disappointing results: Leeds 96, Redruth 6 and Leeds 84, Redruth 24. The first game was in the Pilkington Cup, the second in Courage League Division Three. The clubs may have been in the same division but Redruth, the highest-ranked team in Cornwall, were no match for the nouveaux-riches Yorkshiremen who had become one of England's wealthiest clubs following the £2.25 million sale of their old ground at Kirkstall two years earlier.

Redruth suffered many such embarrassing results during the season. And Peter Johnson, their director of rugby, has a bucketload of reasons why. A former teacher at Colston's School, Bristol's famous rugby academy, Johnson once played in the centre for Bristol and Clifton and for Gloucestershire. In his third season with Redruth, he sees the problems of Cornish rugby clearly and objectively. Johnson's views are pretty damning and would not go down too well in the saloon bars and clubhouses of his adopted county.

There is a story behind those two dreadful results in the space of eight days in Yorkshire. 'Our problem is one of location,' he states rather obviously. 'We have 15 away matches and our nearest away league match is at Exeter, 100 miles and two hours away. We have to make seven trips to Yorkshire. In the autumn the Pilkington Cup regulations had put us in the northern section of the draw. I had a player rebellion on my hands when Redruth were drawn out of the hat to play away at Leeds a week before we played them in the league. It was a nightmare, I can tell you that, and in the end we sent two separate teams.'

Redruth have 44 registered players, 24 of whom are married, and Johnson says that even training twice a week and playing away matches takes its toll on the domestic life of still-amateur players. For their away trips the players disappear on Friday afternoons and arrive home 48 hours later. 'The nature of the players' work also makes life difficult. Many are employed in service industries, as firemen, policemen, paramedics and doctors. They form about a quarter of the squad and are on shift work. They find it difficult turning up to training twice a week and getting Saturdays off. Only ten of the 25 in the first-team squad can train twice a week and be available on Saturdays. Of that ten we've had five long-term injuries.'

Johnson has, therefore, tried to recruit players to Redruth to bolster his first team. 'But Cornwall is a very parochial area. There's a thinly spread population. Village hates village. In Camborne they don't eat red apples because of the association with Redruth. There are stories of people actually riding on the train from Camborne to Bristol and turning the other way when they pass Redruth. Club loyalty is very strong in the county and it's been bred into generations of rugby players. I had a player who came to me two and a half years ago when I went down to Redruth and he was beaten up for coming to the club. His car was destroyed and his house attacked.'

The County Championship, Johnson feels, is another problem. 'The feeling towards it is extremely strong and the height of ambition for many players is to play for Cornwall. Some of those players are happy to stay in the comfort-zone with their own clubs and play for Cornwall five times a year. Another problem is the economy of Cornwall. If you are in an affluent area, a professional rugby club should do well. Here the tin-mining industry has gone, the fishing industry is in ruins. Cornwall has one of the highest unemployment rates in Europe, and one of the lowest average wages. People leave the county to get jobs. I had a player who was in the marketing industry. He was offered a similar job at twice the salary somewhere else. He stayed, I don't know why.

'And now rugby union has gone professional, players can earn money playing the game elsewhere. I lost two players to Gloucester last year. Those guys would have stayed but they can earn more money playing for Gloucester than they would have just from farm labouring. So what's the solution? Well, at the beginning of the season the players met and I asked them to discuss the issue about being paid to play. The players decided that the honour of playing for Redruth was enough. They didn't want to be paid. It was quite significant that the drive to pay them came from the officials largely because the results weren't coming in. So the officials said, "Here is the money to pay the players a £50 win bonus a game." I told them that this wasn't the answer and that the players were playing at the top of their game anyway. Paying them a £50 win bonus wasn't going to make them stronger, faster or fitter. The players themselves were happy that the officials had made the gesture but they didn't want the money. In fact, they regarded it as something of an insult.

'What we have done is introduce a scheme whereby players get £25 for each night they spend away from home while on these difficult away trips. But the players found that £50 for a weekend away didn't make up for the loss of earnings, not an iota of difference. So the club has given me money to actively recruit players and pay them. Where does that money come from? From bars, the gate, programmes, raffles and sponsorship. We've got £20,000 from the local brewery this season. But the financial outlook looks pretty bleak and we're taking a bit of a gamble. We're taking a gamble because if we stay in the Third Division the belief is that money will be forthcoming from Twickenham from Sky deals. I hope the gamble works for my sake and for the sake of Redruth.' The gamble did not work, however. By the end of the season Redruth were relegated and Johnson, for all his missionary work in the duchy, was shown the door.

Redruth's traditional rivals Camborne staged the season's County Championship semi-final against Cumbria on the day of Redruth's vital League Three meeting with Exeter. Camborne, a grey-looking town, was once the centre of the mining industry. Many of the club's early players were miners and the largest and richest mine in the county was Dolcoath. From its 425 fathoms those miners would emerge to play their rugby on Saturday afternoons a century ago. Today the mines have gone, but five of the team that took on Cumbria are farmers. Two-thirds of the team are from Launceston, the Cornish All Blacks who are moving onwards and upwards towards the Courage National Leagues with some trepidation.

But Camborne's ground, far from being set in the bleak, evocative terrain of a dying industrial area, is down a leafy suburban road and adjacent to a pleasant municipal park. Only the sound of seagulls reminds you that you are not in the Home Counties or somewhere in the prosperous rural English Midlands. And the other reminder is inside the ground. On the grassy banks around the pitch and in the stand are 9,000 Cornish supporters, a sea of gold and black. Kilted men bang drums rather tunelessly. A giant pasty hangs from one of the crossbars. Trelawny's sleeping army has awoken.

The game itself, though, is won, and deservedly so, by Cumbria. The 38–24 scoreline and 4–2 try count is a fair reflection of the match. Cumbria had only ever won one county final, as Cumberland and Westmoreland in 1924, and their adventurous display is a fitting tribute to their county chairman Alec Bleasdale, who had died a few weeks earlier. The match is controlled by Cumbria's No. 8 and captain Mark Richardson, whose ample girth is no concession to these days of interactive rugby but who, like Dean Richards, seems to have an uncanny idea of where the ball is going and is not going to waste energy in getting to it. Cumbria win quicker ball and their two centres Paul Burns and Matt Lynch, contracted to rugby league clubs Workington and Carlisle, know how to use it.

Cornwall and Cumbria, England's two most isolated rugby counties, still value the County Championship. The only time Richardson had been at Twickenham was to watch the 1991 World Cup final. 'The win is brilliant for Cumbrian rugby. The County Championship has been demerited but there'll always be a place for it,' says Richardson. The only Redruth players in the Cornwall team are the centre pairing of Kevin Thomas and Ben Stafford, who find their opposite numbers a bit of a handful. Cornwall are disappointed but after the game their players and the Cumbrian victors at least seem to be enjoying themselves in the Camborne clubhouse bar and at the dinner in nearby St Ives. And in these days, when leading players see games as just another day in the office, there is something quite refreshing about that. The only consolation for Trelawny's army is that Redruth have lost. Typically, that news is greeted with unashamed glee.

On the weekend of Redruth's and Cornwall's defeats, though, is another result hiding away in the six-point type of the results section in the sports pages. Combe Down 3, Penzance/Newlyn 93. In Courage South-West Two the Pirates of Penzance are plundering some useful scores, and this was a club record. Penzance are riding on a crest of a small wave thanks to an investment by a millionaire backer, and it is here at the southern-most point of the Cornish peninsula that a future investment may be a salvation for the game in the duchy. That week in the House of Lords, peers from all sides debated the fragile economy of the county. They insisted that schemes such as the projected university at Penzance were vital. Cornwall has no university or college of further education. A university would be an important cradle for talent and it would help keep talented young players within Cornwall.

Peter Johnson may paint a bleak picture of Cornwall, with its insularity and cussedness. Delving back into the past, Roy Standring, a reporter who used to cover the patch for *The Daily Telegraph*, has fonder memories of that insularity. Reporting once on a match at the Memorial Ground in Penryn, he stopped his car when he came upon a gateman. 'That'll be two bob,' said the gateman. 'Sorry,' said Standring, rather too patronisingly for his own good. 'I'm from *The Telegraph*. I'm reporting.' Fumbling for some loose change, Standring then said, 'But I'll have a programme, please.' To which the disapproving old retainer replied, 'Right then, me 'andsome, programmes are five bob.'

So mortified, apparently, were the Penryn committee that they wrote a letter of apology, hoping Standring had not taken offence. He had not. The tale told by the English outsider merely illustrates the Cornish as they are, down-to-earth and not impressed by any metropolitan ways. When I visited Camborne, the people were friendly and unpretentious and certainly not impressed by a reporter from a national newspaper. They were just faintly amused that I had bothered to travel all the way to watch their team.

Bert Solomon was the legend of Cornish rugby. He scored the only try in that Olympic Games defeat by Australia. Solomon was an enigmatic figure, even by Cornish standards. He was also the greatest centre of his day, but he played only once for England, in the 11–6 defeat of Wales at Twickenham in 1910. The Redruth player travelled to London on the milk-train, played brilliantly in the first defeat of Wales this century and, apparently, after the game announced, 'That's it, I've finished.' He ignored Twickenham's future invitations to play, the First World War came and went and Solomon never represented England again. It was said he did not like the haughty English public-school attitudes of some of his new international team-mates. Some said he felt out of place at the after-match dinner. Whatever, Solomon was his own man and he'd be damned if he was going to play for England again. And in one of the earliest examples of cross-border raiding by rugby league, it was also said that this Jeremy Guscott of his day was offered 400 gold sovereigns to go north. Solomon refused what must have been a fortune. One senses that if Rob Andrew had been recruiting for Newcastle in those days he would have been searching for Bert Solomon's mobile phone number. And awkward old Bert would still have elected to stay in his Redruth butcher's shop.

The history of Cornish rugby is littered with tales of these singular men. But while it was the constant threat of water that those old tin-miners were battling against, today it is professionalism that is helping erode the spirit of the game west of the Tamar Bridge. Which is a pity, because there is a uniqueness about Cornish rugby, and because it matters to people there. One only had to see the gold-and-black hordes file out of the Camborne ground on that spring day, silent and resigned that they were not going to return to Twickenham that year, to realise how much it means to them.

That weekend, the local newspapers, radio and TV stations made much of the game, a match largely ignored by the national media. On the evening of the match the local BBC TV news devoted as much time to the game as to what could have been a catastrophic rail accident at Newton Abbot, a derailing that disrupted all the weekend trains in and out of the duchy. But after the rugby preview, you discovered why Cornwall was making such a fuss. The next two sports items were devoted to stock-car racing and land yachting. Outside rugby, naming ten famous Cornish sportsmen is about as difficult as naming ten famous Belgians. Looking out to the sea from Zennor, Perranporth and Padstow, you realise you are on the very edge of England. Next stop America. Rugby union is keeping Cornish sport on the map. What a pity if its great traditions were to drift away on an ebbtide like the Cornish language.

CHAPTER TEN

Visions of Power

In a converted church in Camden the production team of *Rugby Special* is holding its editorial meeting for the following weekend. Wasps could be securing their title at Northampton so they'll be covering that, along with the West Country derby between Gloucester and Bristol. Both teams are in a state of flux and some of Bristol's stars could be moving on if they are relegated. There is also the SWALEC Cup final in Wales and Joel Stransky will be a studio guest. Cardiff Arms Park is to hold an auction to sell off its memorabilia. Someone suggests buying a piece of turf and bringing it to the studio. 'Well, we've had a few sods on the programme this season.'

The mood at the meeting is light-hearted but fatalistic. There are only three more Sundays to prepare for and the atmosphere is like that of a group of clever pupils about to take exams, break up and go their separate ways for a long summer holiday. Gerard Lane, the editor, is the kindly master in charge and John Inverdale is his head boy, already darkly tanned, and chipping in with clever ideas.

Inverdale has been smoothly presenting *Rugby Special* for three years. But not for long. For these are the offices of Chrysalis, the independent production company which also screens Italian soccer on Channel Four and Formula One for ITV but whose three-year contract to screen *Rugby Special* is about to run out. Inverdale, with his bottomless wardrobe of colourful rugby shirts, has become almost as identifiable a rugby voice as Bill McLaren. But BSkyB has secured the rights to show rugby in England and for the first time in 32 years there is to be no magazine called *Rugby Special*.

So fast-moving has this tale of telly folk been in three years that it is difficult to imagine the furore that *Rugby Special* and its casually dressed presenter made when it first came on the air. For in most of those previous 29 years *Rugby Special*, it has to be said, was rather staid and starchy.

'In our first six months we had a pretty big postbag,' remembers Lane. 'And the majority were letters of complaint. John and his rugby shirts were supposed to give the programme a new look but most of the letters – and they were from older viewers, you could tell that – bemoaned the departure of Chris Rea and Ian Robertson. Those viewers were not really accustomed to change and new ideas. They wanted men in suits to present the programme. But often, in those days, that programme would consist of two matches and one of them would be some game in the Borders watched by three men and a dog. There was also a minority of letters in those early days saying how refreshing it was.'

Twickenham, good old progressive Twickenham, had stipulated that an independent company should produce *Rugby Special*. The Rugby Football Union wanted a programme that would effectively be a shop-window to sell the game, a livelier magazine programme with a fixed time when rugby followers would be indoors and not playing or in their local. And so from Chrysalis flew *Rugby Special* with its stirring theme tune, its jazzy graphics, its often glut of highlights, its intelligent analysis and its array of guests, the players black-eyed but bright as buttons, the not-so-ashen-faced managers and coaches. And in the middle of it all, Inverdale, with his clubhouse *bonhomie* but not averse to a little Paxmanesque probing.

Talking of probing, there was an earlier controversial guest appearance of Jeff Probyn, the former England prop, who poured scorn on the women's game and added to the letters in Gerard Lane's postbag. There was also an appearance by Sid Going, the taciturn old All Blacks scrum-half, who didn't appear to have any views on anything. *Rugby Special* was not afraid to show the seamier side of the game, the citings, the sly off-the-ball punches and kicks, and it broke stories such as that special general meeting in Birmingham on the Sunday afternoon in early 1996 when most of us were caught off-guard by the backwoodsmen who revolted against the very idea of a professional game.

According to Lane, 'The programme used to be a lot different. It was not so much a magazine and there was no attempt to analyse. But the times were different. Rugby was not on the back pages of newspapers in those days. Sky are the paymasters now. It's a pity for us because we were just getting our teeth into the subject and I'm disappointed we can't continue. We had become pretty well known among the clubs and the players. We've done a lot to raise the profile of the players and helped continue the debate in the game. Occasionally we get letters wondering why there is not too much Scottish and Welsh rugby and it has been seen as an English-biased programme. But the standard of rugby is now so much better in England and the Courage League, and the Scots and Welsh have their own programmes. And John Inverdale has put his stamp on the programme. He is a massive rugby fan, not just a TV presenter. He's not someone you have to handle with care.'

The modern-day *Rugby Special* has attracted an audience that has averaged around 1.4 million, a respectable following, and in recent years the game has become attractive to commercial broadcasters who saw they could secure advertising revenue from those A and B viewers. But it was the arrival on the scene of Rupert Murdoch's BSkyB that further revolutionised the small-screen coverage of the game and in the summer of 1996 brought England to the brink of a civil war with its partners in the Five Nations Championship. In the stampede to gain the TV rights into the next century, the terrestrial channels were left buried at the bottom of a muddy ruck while the big money enabled Sky to run away with the ball.

The securing of television rights became the major issue

between Twickenham, its leading clubs and the champion of the grass-roots Cliff Brittle, the chairman of the RFU's executive committee. On a Monday morning in June the nation's attentions were concentrated on Euro 96 and the prospects of Terry Venables and his boys when news from Twickenham elbowed Gazza and his friends off the back pages. The Rugby Football Union announced a unilateral £87.5 million deal with BSkyB for exclusive rights to all international, club and representative games in England. The deal would allow a terrestrial broadcaster, probably the BBC whose three-year £27 million contract was to run out at the end of the 1996–97 season, the right to broadcast internationals 'as live' not less than two hours after the games had been shown.

For Brittle, who had been elected as chairman that January, the deal was beyond the pale. He had been excluded from the TV talks and reacted in typical fashion, claiming, 'In my view, democracy no longer prevails within the RFU. The TV negotiators have taken a quick fix and not taken the long-term future of the game into consideration.' But it was the reaction of England's home nations partners – France had their own domestic TV deal – that caused Twickenham the problems. The Celts went ballistic. All summer a battle raged every bit as rumbustious as a game at Lansdowne Road or Murrayfield. England were portrayed as running roughshod over their partners, who threatened a Four Nations tournament without them.

Earlier that month Sky had negotiated an astronomic TV deal for Premiership soccer worth £670 million. It was now offering Wales a quite generous £40 million for its games and Scotland and Ireland £18 million each for its matches. 'I would like to make it clear to the RFU that this decision will jeopardise matches at all age-group levels, not just full international matches. They will also have difficulties finding match officials,' warned Fred McLeod, Scotland's representative on the Five Nations Committee.

The RFU's stance was that it had to fund a professional game and had an outstanding loan of £34 million to pay off for the rebuilding of Twickenham. Those were the cold facts from its then treasurer David Robinson, but Wales, Scotland and Ireland did not see things like that. They thought the heritage of the Five Nations was not Twickenham's to sell off. Yes, they may have had a legal right, but surely not a moral one. We're in this together, they argued.

And so Euro 96 came and went, and so did the cricketers of India and Pakistan, the golfers of the Open and the tennis players of Wimbledon. The domestic season was under way before Colin Herridge, one of England's negotiators in the summer TV talks, dramatically brandished his piece of paper at a publisher's launch of the new *Rothman's Rugby Union Yearbook* in central London in September and said, 'We have peace in our time.' The world's oldest rugby union tournament, and the bedrock of the game in the Northern Hemisphere, had been saved after all-night talks at the then headquarters of the International Board in Bristol, but England had been forced to agree that most of the money go into a communal pot. England had also agreed not to negotiate separately for the rights to broadcast Five Nations matches when the deal expired in 2002. Now 90 per cent of the TV income would be split between the participating countries and prize money would be introduced for the competition.

Looking back at the end of the season, Tony Hallett, the RFU secretary and one of England's other TV negotiators, told me, 'There'll be opportunities for clubs, schools and our members to participate in heavily subsidised dishes, decoders and rentals to allow them to watch rugby in the future. Sky's audience levels for their Saturday afternoon rugby have gone up from around 100,000 to 450,000. That's a remarkable growth. A lot of clubhouses have dishes and their spectator numbers have grown. I hope there'll be some provision for *Rugby Special*. We've done all in our power to encourage it. There will be more Sunday coverage of rugby matches in the future and when you combine that with repeated satellite coverage there will be more rugby on television than ever.

'All sections of the game will benefit from Sky's £87.5 million. Of this around £60 million will be available for rugby below the levels of League One and Two. There will be youth programmes for schools and insurance schemes. The County Championship

111

will continue and there will be student liaison officers to make sure that the pipeline of talent from universities is left open. We're concerned that players leave schools for universities and drift away from the game. None of the things we wanted would have been possible without that TV investment.'

But, having solved a domestic crisis over TV rights in that long, hot summer, the battleground shifted to Europe during the autumn. The Heineken European Cup kicked off in October 1996, the second season of the competition but the first with English clubs in tow. It was the biggest club competition in the Northern Hemisphere and there were some marvellous matches in the early stages, but ITV, who were to have covered the competition, pulled the plug on its coverage, fed up with the wrangling between the organisers. The competition was the responsibility of the European Rugby Cup organisation, basically the same Five Nations Committee that had been negotiating during the summer. Meanwhile, the European clubs wanted to forge separate TV deals and formed an umbrella group, the European Rugby Federation. ERF asked for tenders from television companies to broadcast an extended European League and Cup event to begin in the autumn of 1997.

ERF's plans were pretty revolutionary. Apart from this Super League it wanted to scrap the Pilkington Cup and revamp the Courage leagues. The clubs in Courage League Two would now make up the leading division in England and from there there would be promotion to two European pools. In ERF's brave new world the fixtures people wanted to see were Bath versus Toulouse or Wasps versus Treviso, not Bath versus Orrell or Wasps versus West Hartlepool.

But BSkyB eventually did a deal with ERC for the European Cup instead, and any hopes the clubs had for a Super League, with rights negotiated through the clubs themselves and not the unions, were strangled at birth. BSkyB was not interested in dealing with renegade clubs and asked the English clubs to heal their rift with Twickenham. Sky wanted the guaranteed release of players from the clubs to England teams because they did not want their future contract with Twickenham threatened. The clubs ultimately found themselves in a corner.

And so television eventually played the leading role in forcing the English clubs, and its umbrella organisation the English Professional Rugby Union Clubs, to come back to the negotiating table. Without the TV money the clubs could not contemplate breaking away from their unions and forging that separate commercial identity.

Sky's winning of the television rights to the sport in England will change the culture of watching the Five Nations. No more cosy afternoons in front of *Grandstand*. More rugby followers will be enticed to clubhouses and pubs to watch the games in winter if they don't have match tickets. As far as Twickenham is concerned, the closing of the wider shop-window to the game is compensated for by the amount of money that will flow into the shop. But the Sky deal further eroded the notion of free access to major domestic sporting events. There are 'listed' events such as Wimbledon, the Grand National and the FA Cup final, but a Labour government is hardly going to make adding rugby union to those events a top priority.

The alternative view to Twickenham and the paymasters of Sky is that it was the terrestrial televising of the World Cups and international matches that created the upsurge of interest in the game in the first place. But the very size of the BSkyB cheque meant that that view was ultimately of no currency by the time television negotiations were being hammered out. In an ideal world the domestic contract would have stayed with the BBC, we could have listened to Bill McLaren for ever and the home unions would still have lots of money to spend on nurturing the game. But, as the production team at Chrysalis discovered, nothing in the 1996–97 season was standing still.

CHAPTER ELEVEN

Losing Track

Not for nothing is Olivier Merle, the lock forward whose rumbustious play helped France to their 1997 Grand Slam, known in his native land as 'the Diceman'. The man-mountain from Grenoble, who has also been given the soubriquet of 'L'homme et demi' back home, was once one of his country's leading shot-putters. With his eye on a career change, Merle was once with some friends in a Grenoble bar. 'I'll throw this dice and if it lands on six, I'll play rugby,' said our hero. *Et Voilà*. Now we have the pleasure of watching Merle on the rugby fields of Europe.

But as rugby union has turned professional and the popularity of track and field in Britain has slumped, the fear of athletics at home is that many more career-minded athletes will be hoping to land on the six. Martin Watkins coaches two of Britain's leading 400 metres runners Mark Hilton and Mark Richardson. He also used to coach Ian McLaughlin, the most promising of the country's hammer-throwers. McLaughlin was on the verge of becoming a junior international when, at 19, he signed to play rugby for Harlequins. McLaughlin was given a bursary by Quins to study Russian and Law at Guildford University. He was happy to play second-team rugby where his profile was no greater or no less than that of a junior hammer-thrower.

'He would have made the England team for the next Commonwealth Games,' says Watkins, who sells computer systems by day and in the evenings coaches at the Windsor, Slough and Eton club. 'But he's now earning a wage and getting well coached. Athletics could not compete with that. Mark Hilton is one of our leading runners but he's had to go to California for warm-weather training and pay for it himself. When Mark Richardson was studying at Loughborough he used to commute to Windsor. Ian is a hammer-thrower and that's an event that is well down the queue when the money's being handed out.

'I think rugby has it just about right in that it is paying its leading players and the rest of the game is amateur. I also think it will continually take away a good percentage of our talent. Athletics will continue to be a breeding-ground for rugby union. If I were a recruiting agent for rugby I would look at the big men doing these heavyweight events like the discus and the hammer. And athletics has its ten-step scheme in which it teaches youngsters all the rudimentary skills like running, jumping and throwing, and they learn the co-ordination necessary for rugby.'

The Dublin-born McLaughlin left Harlequins midway through the season after winning a place in the Ireland Under-21 squad and joined London Irish, where he trained with Margot Wells, wife of the former Olympic sprint champion Allan. He had played rugby at RGS High Wycombe, a school that has recently produced England internationals Matthew Dawson and Nick Beal, and won a place in the England Under-16 side. As he explained, 'I started hammer-throwing at 15 and for two years my parents would take me to West London Stadium to train three or four times a week. But I received no financial backing and none was really in the offing. I'm under contract at Irish and hope to make a career here. I really can't see myself going back to athletics. And I'm sure rugby will look to throwers and jumpers to recruit in future.'

McLaughlin may not have been a regular name on the back pages but Jason John was the most high-profile of the early athletes to follow in the boot steps of Will Carling rather than Linford Christie. Around the time Christie was throwing away his spikes in a rubbish bin at the Atlanta Olympics, Jason John was swapping his for a pair of rugby boots and a career at League Two club Moseley, the sleeping giants of Midlands rugby. John was the man Christie had tipped to become his eventual successor and four months before he turned his back on athletics he was Britain's most successful sprinter at the European Indoor Athletics Championships in Stockholm, where he won a silver medal. He said he had more security in rugby union and, having played at junior level, was confident of making the transition.

'I know people in track and field who are struggling to pay their next mortgage cheque. Rugby has offered me a wage and a car and pays my medical expenses,' he said. But Moseley struggled to hold on to their League Two status during the season. John struggled too, finding blinding pace was not enough to elude predatory tacklers. By the end of the season their star turn was not even a regular name in the first team.

In Wales, John's dubious ranking as the fastest man in British rugby was challenged by Peter Maitland, a lower-profile signing by Bridgend. Maitland put his athletics career on hold after just missing out on a place in Britain's 100 metres relay squad in Atlanta. His personal best for the 100 metres was 10.42 seconds, and at 15 stone, defences found he took some stopping. He was called into a Wales sevens squad after only two games of senior rugby for Cardiff the previous season, but Cardiff failed to pursue the man who had run for Wales in the Commonwealth Games in 1994. Maitland did not force his way into the Bridgend first team, though, and when winter set in he switched codes to join Salford Reds of the Super League.

John and Maitland were following a trend set by Nigel Walker, an Olympic hurdler who switched to rugby union before it turned professional and ended up on the wing for Wales. Walker's scintillating try against Swansea helped Cardiff to their victory in the SWALEC Cup final in April 1997, emphasising his talent and making one wonder why he was being ignored by Wales. Swansea's coach Mike Ruddock could only watch and admire as Walker eluded four tackles and kept his balance to weave down the left wing for one of the best scores seen in Wales all season, a try which brought the curtain down on the Arms

Park in appropriately spectacular fashion. 'Sprinters like Wells and Christie have both won medals in their thirties,' he said. 'Walker is still fit and fast and will probably be around for the 1999 World Cup.'

'I turned to rugby in September 1992,' says Walker. 'I was 29 and had just failed to make it to the Olympics when I came fifth in the trials. I knew I wasn't going to go any further in international athletics and rugby had been my first love. I had played at school until I was 18 and then made a choice to become a full-time athlete. At that time I wanted a sport in which you could measure how good you were and things weren't subjective.

'When I came back to rugby there wasn't a Ieuan Evans or a Gerald Davies around on the left wing, so I saw there was an opening in the international side. The laws had changed in the meantime. Rugby had become more of a 15-man game and I had to relearn skills. You needed to be physically faster and stronger. Athletics is in a trough at the moment and the money is a big carrot. There were vast amounts of money for the leading athletes when I was in the sport, while even if you were a British Lion you'd only be playing for beer money. Now the sports have passed each other like ships in the night. If you are an international athlete you could be running or jumping for nothing, but even an ordinary club rugby player can be earning a living from the game.

'Now 16, 17 and 18-year-olds are being faced with a stark choice. Do I carry on throwing the javelin or jumping over hurdles or do I aim to be a good club rugby player? There are more and more sports available for teenagers and it will be a dogfight to gain their attention. I can see rugby clubs looking to field athletes for their forwards, and speed is always going to be a valuable commodity. If you can catch the ball and run like the wind, you will obviously have a big advantage.'

Athletics also lost a prestigious talent in Paul Sampson, the Yorkshire schoolboy famously summoned to his headmaster's office at the beginning of 1996 and instead of being given the expected dressing-down was told he had been called up for an England training squad. Sampson completed his A-level studies and won the English Schools sprint title with some ease before

117

giving athletics the hand-off and signing professional forms for Wasps. The club found him a flat in south-west London and he continued his studies at university. As Sampson helped lay the European champions Toulouse to waste in that memorable 77–17 win at Loftus Road, as he outpaced Jeremy Guscott for a try that sank the league champions Bath at the Recreation Ground, and as he worked his way into the England A team, Wasps consider this was one of their sounder investments.

At a more modest level Derek Redmond, Mr Sharron Davies and a former 400 metres record-holder, began playing for Stow-on-the-Wold in South-West Division's Southern Counties North. Elliot Bunney, a former European junior 100 metres champion, has been cutting a dash for Heriot's FP, one of Scotland's leading clubs. He had changed sports in 1994, finding it difficult to motivate himself for athletics once he realised he was not going to be the next Linford Christie. Unlike John, Bunney, whose father was a former Scottish trialist, has had little trouble in switching sports. The wing forced his way into the Edinburgh side during the 1996–97 season and Gavin Hastings, who played for Watsonians in a fixture against Heriot's during the Christmas break, felt the force of one of his tackles.

Richard Simmons, the chief sprint coach for the British Athletic Federation, says he is concerned for the future of his sport. 'It's obviously attractive to someone from school to join a rugby club, even a middle-ranking club like Reading or Newbury, and earn a living. No athletics club could afford to pay them and I think Jason John has discovered that training for rugby is a lot easier than training for athletics. Sprinters are obviously going to be in demand from rugby clubs but field athletes, too, are often attractive. Abi Ekoku used to be a discus-thrower. He played rugby for Blackheath as an amateur but now he's making a living out of rugby league at Bradford. Yes, it is a concern, but at the end of the day we have to compete with all sports. In the future, well, it's not up to me to say, but I don't see how rugby clubs who bring in a few hundred spectators can generate enough money to pay these players in the long term.'

The much-lamented Ron Pickering once said athletics in Britain had '15 millionaires and 15,000 paupers'. Pickering saw professionalism in athletics as a curse and urged rugby union not to give up its amateur status. Whether Pickering's bleak scenario can be applied to rugby union remains to be seen, but what the coach and commentator could not have predicted was that when it did turn professional, so many athletes would opt to take the money and run.

CHAPTER TWELVE

Upwardly Mobile

The Newbury News of 7 February 1970 was scathing. Beneath the headline 'Rugby Players Must Train Harder' its sports editor thundered, 'Of the 23 matches played so far, Newbury 1st XV have won 15, drawn one and lost nine. In their remaining 11 fixtures they face several strong teams and the present pattern is likely to continue unless they can buckle down to some serious tactical training. At present the Tuesday night training sessions are, on average, attended by no more than 15 enthusiasts and of those only John Golding and John Maylen from the first XV regularly support them.'

Well, John Golding and John Maylen wouldn't recognise the Newbury first team today from their idle team-mates of 27 years ago. In fact, they wouldn't recognise the club. It has moved just half a mile up Monks Lane, on the south side of the prosperous Berkshire town. The two Johns probably wouldn't recognise Newbury if they had been transported in a time machine to the present day. Thames Valley became Silicon Valley during the '80s and the new industries on the other side of town have transformed the once-sedate place known for its racecourse and not much else.

'The Thatcherite town of the '80s' is what Terry Burwell, the club's director of rugby, calls Newbury. It is an apt description, and in the new market-forces of rugby union Newbury are being swept upwards and upwards through the Courage League like some blue tornado. Newbury are dominating Courage League Four South just as Worcester are cutting a swath through League Four North. In Tony Blair's new Britain they have become rugby's new middle classes.

Terry Burwell once played in the centre at Leicester, for whom he performed in two John Player Cup finals. He became director of rugby at Newbury in 1989 when professionalism was just a twinkle in the eye of one of Burwell's former Leicester team-mates Peter Wheeler, who was to be in the vanguard of talks between the leading clubs and Twickenham. At that time Newbury were already negotiating to sell their ground for development to Sainsbury's. The club eventually received over £4 million for the site, then found a fallow field nearby, and in October 1996 a new home opened and Newbury were off and running.

The £3.75 million Newbury Sports Arena is the model new-age rugby club. Traditionalists may carp that it lacks the ambience of the beery old rugger club, but if ambience is being crushed in the tobacco fog of a bar where the only food is a packet of pork scratchings, good riddance ambience. Newbury welcome families. In fact, there are enough toddlers in the non-smoking section of the bar to play an Under-threes match before the first-team fixture against Berry Hill that afternoon. They actually serve cappuccino behind the bar, but they probably serve Calpol too. Upstairs you can have a slice of lime in your gin and tonic. That's how upmarket Newbury are.

In the club's programme and around the first-team pitch there are more adverts than in *Exchange and Mart*. Terry Burwell admits, 'Some people may say we're too overtly commercial, but we're also very much part of the community here and we're not just concerned with the welfare of the first team. This weekend 350 players will be pulling on a Newbury shirt. In the Christmas term all the schools in the area have used the pitches here to play rugby.' Burwell stands on the balcony of the new grandstand, half an hour before the first team play Berry Hill in their 14th

Courage League fixture of the season. Newbury have won all of their 13 previous games. Berry Hill, a village team from the Forest of Dean, know that keeping the score to reasonable proportions will be enough for them this afternoon. The club where Dennis Potter once strutted his stuff as a three-quarter don't even have a stand. At Berry Hill spectators stand around the touchline with a pint, and Dennis Potter would have approved of a distinct lack of cappuccino in the bar.

From where Burwell stands, the new club looks a picture. Its model is the natural bowl of Pontypool, the Welsh ground surrounded by huge grassy banks. There are four other pitches around the first-team arena. The ground opened in the autumn of 1996 with a league match against local rivals Henley. Old scores were settled with an 11–9 victory. Watching the game was Chalkie White, the South-west selector and coaching guru. White was keeping a careful eye on Brian Johnson, the Newbury wing who had already forced his way into the England A team. A month later Johnson scored a try when the ground was officially launched with a match against the touring Western Samoans. Newbury lost 35–21 but, on a freezing evening, probably performed better than Ireland, who suffered the first of their five home defeats of their dreadful season when they also lost to the tourists.

Three months on, Newbury beat Berry Hill 34–0. When John McCartney, Newbury's blind-side flanker, scores a try after four minutes, someone mutters, 'The first of many.' They're spoilt at Newbury nowadays. Berry Hill are content to spoil, keep the game tight and hope that Johnson doesn't see too much of the ball. He sees enough to score three nicely executed tries, but the performance of Newbury, who aim to play an expansive game, is perfunctory. 'Our worst of the season,' says Burwell.

Burwell has recruited Keith Richardson, the Geordie who has coached Gloucester and, more recently, Harlequins, and who has also helped forge a successful England A team. Richardson, a former teacher, coaches here twice a week. 'I would hate to be a full-time professional. There's more to life,' he says. 'But this club are a pleasure to work for. People think we've scoured the country for players but they've actually come here. Last summer five players – the Osman brothers, Tim, Russell and Nick – turned up from Southampton, while Andy Duke and Tom Holloway also just turned up. Four of them are in the first team today. The players themselves are still the best recruiting agents.'

Newbury's first-teamers earn, on average, around £5,000 a year on a pay-for-play basis. Some, like one of the club's few big names, Colin Hall, earn more. Hall, a lock, has come to Newbury via Northampton and London Irish and his nous in the pack is invaluable to a young side. Some of the players opt to drive a club car rather than receive the cash. But Newbury know their place. There is good husbandry on this former farmland, and there are no big-name foreign imports just yet. 'Some clubs were professional in many ways before 1995,' says Burwell. 'But the word "professional" means a lot of different things. As we see it, it doesn't just mean being paid for something. It means being commercial. We've planned a long time for this season. We own the ground but we don't have a benefactor to fall back on, so we have to be businesslike.'

Newbury may not have a sugar-daddy but they have a host of sponsors to pay the wage bills. Vodafone, the town's biggest employer, have pumped in around £100,000. Newbury are also trying to emulate Worcester by building an indoor training centre on their site and are hoping that a £2.4 million bid to the National Lottery will provide that floodlit facility. But, in the meantime, promotion to League Three will do nicely. Newbury's League Three neighbours Reading received some £70,000 from Twickenham for being in the Third Division last season, ten times more than the League Four clubs received. Berry Hill, meanwhile, are quite content with their £7,000. Their treasurer admits that Newbury are a model club, but his committee colleagues also admit that they won't mind seeing the back of these new kids on the block.

The taxi driver who picks me up from the ground is from Montana but has lived here for 18 years. Yes, he says, the town is unrecognisable from when he first came here. 'But this club seem to have put the place on the map,' he says. 'There isn't a lot to do here if you don't like horse-racing. But it's given the area a bit of a lift. I might even go to watch them myself some day.'

Newbury will soon have its controversial bypass, and a lot of rugby followers seem destined to turn off towards the Sports Arena in the coming years.

Near Junction 6 off the M5, another aspiring club are moving into the fast lane. Worcester have been playing rugby union since 1871, when the Reverend Francis John Ed founded the club who played their first game against Worcester Artillery. But it is fair to say that for a century and a quarter, Worcester have not been at the cutting edge of the sport. They have been just another club happy to cruise in the middle lane. Until now. Step forward Cecil Duckworth, local multi-millionaire and Worcester supporter since he moved to the city 40 years ago.

Duckworth made his fortune selling his successful heating business. Now he has ambitions to make Worcester one of Europe's top clubs. Snigger not, for Toulouse, Cardiff and Bath could be turning off the M5 and heading towards Sixways before long. The England coach Jack Rowell and his assistant Les Cusworth have already graced Worcester's new-look ground. In December 1996, the pair came to the official opening of an indoor training centre, an amenity Worcester hope will become a centre of excellence and be used by other clubs and schools for winter training. Leicester used the centre during the harsh post-Christmas break to train for their European Cup semi-final when Welford Road was frozen over. Overlooking the centre is a 250-seat lecture theatre.

The second phase of the transformation of Sixways is a restyled clubhouse, 800-seat stadium, corporate hospitality facilities and changing-rooms and bars. These were completed at the end of the 1996–97 season when Worcester, in only their second year in the National League, easily won promotion to League Three along with Newbury. By the end of the summer Worcester had a brand-new floodlit pitch to run out on to in League Three. If and when Worcester are promoted again, there are plans for a 6,000-seat grandstand.

All this is thanks to Cecil Duckworth's injection of £1.3 million and a matching donation from the National Lottery. 'Division One is our aim. Cecil is very ambitious and has the

124

wherewithal to help us reach there,' says Dick Cumming, Worcester's first-team manager. 'We're not a set-up like Gloucester, which is surrounded by junior clubs, but it's a large enough catchment area here with clubs like Kidderminster and Malvern to provide us with players. And the city's two major rugby-playing schools, Royal Grammar School and King's, have each provided us with three past captains and they're all in our first team. Locally we're attracting talented players. They're all part-time players here. Only Tim Smith classes himself as a professional. The younger lads may want to make a career of playing rugby but most are holding on to their careers.'

Smith, a prolific goalkicking full-back, is one of a number of signings from Gloucester that include the scrum-half Bruce Fenley and the forwards Chris Raymond and Peter Miles. The lock Steve Lloyd has joined via Harlequins and Moseley and the wing Barry Evans via Leicester and Coventry. Evans earns around £7,000, plus bonuses and appearance money of around £100 a game. The Gloucester imports mostly earn salaries of between £10,000 and £15,000. As at Newbury, the money is not in the François Pienaar league, but Worcester have concentrated on recruiting good, middle-ranking domestic players rather than foreign mercenaries. And one leading Springbok played for the club long before Pienaar, Stransky and Atherton. Four years earlier, Ruben Kruger, the best open-side flanker in the 1995 World Cup, played for a season at Sixways thanks to a member of Worcester who had contacts in the South African winemaking trade. 'He made a big impression. I wish we could afford to have him back,' laughs Cumming.

Newbury and Worcester, through the sale of land and through the existence of a wealthy benefactor, are beginning to shake up the cosy old order in English rugby union. What they both realise is that they need the backing of local businesses and they need to produce homegrown talent if their upwardly mobile journey through the leagues is to continue. During the 1996–97 season Worcester received a number of job applications from aspiring Australian and South African players. They were not looking for big bucks on the rugby field but for the opportunities of local employment while they played semi-professionally. In a way the freemasonry of rugby has always helped young players find employment. Newbury and Worcester just hope that their state-of-the-art grounds and growing reputations will attract the better quality young players to the Arena and Sixways rather than Welford Road and The Stoop. At the moment Newbury and Worcester are like punters at their local racecourses with money to spend after that successful each-way bet. They both finished the season unbeaten with Newbury winning every league game and passing the 1,000 point mark in the process. But the real challenge will be to attract bigger local audiences in what are not exactly rugby hotbeds. Only then will the likes of Newbury and Worcester evolve from stars of the local rep to major players on the national stage.

CHAPTER THIRTEEN

The Broncos Go Hoarse

The Stoop, a stroll away from Twickenham, was an ironic home for two young rugby players to be sharing at the tail-end of the union season. Adrian Spencer and Steve Pilgrim were the last victims of Twickenham's spiteful former ruling that if you dabbled with rugby league you risked burning bridges with rugby union. The pair didn't so much take the league shilling, though, as opt to do a spot of unpaid work only to finish up with the bill. It seems bizarre now that for exactly 100 years rugby league was able to pour scorn on union for banning players who opted to play the 13-man game, regardless of whether or not they were paid. The scorn was well deserved. But now those bridges have been rebuilt, Adrian Spencer is back at The Stoop, albeit in the red, white and blue of the London Broncos, the south of England standard-bearers in the Super League, and Steve Pilgrim's progress has taken him to Harlequins, where he makes the occasional performance in that club's multi-coloured shirt in the south's more traditional code.

Spencer is a bit of a footnote in the history of rugby union. There he is in the list of Cambridge Blues in *Rothman's Rugby Union Yearbook*, the game's *Wisden*. Spencer A., 1994 (R). The afternoon of 6 December 1994 had seen him granted his 15 minutes of fame – well, 23 actually – as a second-half replacement in a Cambridge side that beat Oxford 26–21. That fame is usually welcome for the student, many of whom reach the zenith of their rugby careers at the Varsity Match and are never heard of again. But for Spencer the spotlight was not so desirable. The rugby league press noticed that this same Spencer A. had played as an amateur for rugby league's London Crusaders two years earlier. All hell broke loose. The blazers at Twickenham did their impression of a crotchety magistrate. Spencer A. was banned for a year.

The ban was cut short when rugby union went professional and the pettiness went out of the window, and in September 1995 Adrian Spencer was playing union again at Cambridge as he embarked upon his fourth and final year in chemical engineering, an appropriate subject for the man from Warrington, the home of the Chemics. 'I don't bear Twickenham any grudges at all,' he says now. 'I can see they had no choice but to ban me. While I was at Cambridge Steve Cottrell, who's now playing for Richmond, helped me out as he was a lawyer, but by the time the 1995–96 season had started Cambridge had been on a pre-season tour to Zimbabwe which I missed out on and I was only a replacement for the 1995 Varsity Match. To be honest, I prefer rugby league. It's the game I was brought up on in Warrington.'

Steve Pilgrim, too, was remarkably unfazed by his ban, which did last a year back in the unenlightened times of 1993–94. 'I'm not bitter at the lost year,' he told me when he did come back to play union. 'I know the RFU could have thrown the book at me. Now I've been given a second chance.' Pilgrim's crime was to go north to play in a trial match as 'A.N. Other' for Leeds against Wakefield Trinity reserves. Again he was spotted by a member of the fourth estate who recognised him from a match he had played for Wasps at West Hartlepool earlier in the season. Pilgrim had worked his way to England A status and had been a member of the England Development squad for the 1995 World Cup. He admitted to being bored with union, and the heavier and heavier demands on still-amateur players were taking their toll.

In the bad old days it was Wales's rugby union side that suffered the greatest erosion of talent that took the northern trail to rugby league. Jonathan Davies, Scott Gibbs, Scott Quinnell, Allan Bateman and Richard Webster were just a handful who disappeared in the '90s. And it was not with the blessing of their clubs. There was often bitterness and recrimination. Famously, when Gibbs departed he was labelled a 'prostitute' by the then Swansea chairman Mike James, who claimed the club had offered Gibbs a generous financial package to stay in Wales. Gibbs replied with a scathing attack on what he claimed was the hypocrisy in the so-called amateur game. 'Every player in Wales knows that when you play on a Saturday, if you win you can get a few quid. Players get the cash after the game. Envelopes are handed round. At some clubs you get a cheque at the end of the week. It's a win bonus,' he told *Rugby World* magazine back in 1994.

This was fairly typical of the level of debate at the time. But now Davies, Gibbs, Quinnell, Bateman and Webster have returned to rugby union, with Gibbs, Quinnell and Bateman fast-tracked back in to the Wales and subsequently the Lions sides. All is sweetness and light, and when two very tired sides, Bath, the champions of union, and Wigan, undisputed masters of rugby league, played their cross-code challenge matches at the end of the 1995–96 season, it was confirmation of bridges mended. In another symbolic gesture, some of the best rugby league players were loaned to union clubs in the autumn of 1996. It was the close season in the summer Super League and a chance for league players to have a holiday job. Harlequins borrowed Gary Connolly from Wigan and Robbie Paul from Bradford Bulls, Paul's elder brother Henry went to Bath along with his Wigan team-mate Jason Robinson, and Va'aiga Tuigamala, a former All Black, returned to the union code, making the biggest impact of all with Wasps.

It was a good bit of public relations but it was an experiment that none of the union clubs said they could afford to repeat. As was seen from Bath's cross-code games with Wigan, with each team easily winning its version of rugby, the sports are vastly different. Robinson thrilled and frustrated supporters at the Recreation Ground. The little wing could be devastating from broken play, twisting and turning out of tackles and scorching down the touchlines. But I remember seeing him play an early game at Gloucester. He picked up a bobbing ball in his 22 and ran straight into two Gloucester forwards, rather than kicking safely to touch. Forgetting how different the tackle law was, Robinson clung on to the ball, the referee awarded a penalty, Gloucester said 'Thanks very much' and Mark Mapletoft kicked the three points.

There were the familiar brickbats from the rugby league die-hards when the five returned for the Super League season and Connolly and Henry Paul hobbled home rather than skipping back north. 'What have you union lot done to Tuigamala?' chided *The Guardian*'s rugby league correspondent Paul Fitzpatrick. 'He looks out of condition and overweight.' 'But good enough to play union' was the inference of that. But the games are radically different. There is no cover defence in rugby league, and although Robbie Paul and Gary Connolly looked irresistible in attack for Quins they had no idea how to defend, and the obvious difference in the tackle law between the two games prevented the new boys from making a major impact. Tuigamala was an exception because he had played union at the very top level. Rugby league is primarily a handling game and the five did show great handling skills, but in the world of the ruck and maul they failed to crack the code.

'As long as the game is marketed properly I don't see why it shouldn't catch on in London, and perhaps people who watch Quins and Richmond and all the clubs in the area during the winter will watch us during the summer,' says Adrian Spencer. 'The codes are no longer in competition. I'm in touch with people I was at university with, friends in the City, people with disposable income, and have been urging them to come along.'

Spencer's optimism is a familiar refrain from rugby followers south of the River Trent who have tried unsuccessfully to spread the gospel of the 13-man game outside its strongholds of Yorkshire, Lancashire and Cumbria. Adrian Spencer is known as 'Adey' Spencer in his rugby league guise – 'Adrian sounds like something my mum might call me when she is cross,' he jokes – and the London Broncos have had a few name changes themselves in their attempt to achieve success in the capital. The

Fulham side which began life at Craven Cottage in 1980 has evolved from the London Crusaders to the Broncos and has trailed around the suburbs of the capital. Crystal Palace, Chiswick, Barnet, Hendon, Brentford and Charlton, the list of homes sounds like an index to an A to Z. There was even a stop at Stamford Bridge and a very brief stay in Widnes. But now the back-packing Broncos have a home. This is their first of three seasons as tenants at a ground that couldn't be closer to the heart of rugby union's establishment. The Stoop, home of Harlequins, has been transformed in the first season of professional rugby union with its spanking new East Stand, and it looks a picture. But it is still dwarfed by the concrete and steel monolith that has risen on the opposite side of Chertsey Road.

This area of south-west London is a bastion of rugby union and if rugby league can put down roots here, it can flourish anywhere. For 17 years rugby league has struggled to sink those roots into London's clay. The Broncos are anxious to be loved but face an eternal struggle to gain coverage in London's newspapers and on London's airwaves. Indeed, you could live in the capital and easily be blissfully unaware of the existence of the London Broncos. Tonight they are playing the Leeds Rhinos in a Super League game at the very untraditional kick-off time of 6.35 on a sunny Sunday evening. Leeds are now Leeds Rhinos, Wigan are Wigan Warriors, Warrington are Warrington Wolves and Oldham are Oldham Bears. Image is all. Not to be stuffy, to appeal to a younger audience and to a wider culture, and to break away from the smokestack images of the industrial North is the goal of Super League. And don't ever mention Eddie Waring.

That afternoon across south London at the Oval, an eight-foot-tall clown wearing an outsize top hat and wheeling around on a Day-Glo yellow scooter cavorted with a Lion-headed clown called Roary. Yes, it was a cricket match: Surrey versus Somerset in the Axa Life League. Surrey took to the pitch to Gothic classical music which developed into Frankie Goes to Holly-wood's 'Two Tribes'. Somerset came out to Reef's 'So Come Back Brighter'. They didn't, as Surrey won by three wickets. I'm not sure if the Bedser twins were in the crowd.

David Gilbert, Surrey's cricket manager, said he had imported the innovations from New Zealand in order to jazz up the Sunday game and attract more followers. 'The innovations will not only attract new crowds and provide family entertainment but will also lift the players either in the middle of or after a hard four-day championship match.' At tea there were coaching sessions at indoor nets, welcome packs featuring colouring-in kits, free magazines and a face painter. All good fun, but enough to make the traditional cricket follower go as white as a pair of flannels.

At The Stoop, Ronnie the Rhino has just attempted to grab one of the passing Crown Jewels. Ronnie is the Leeds mascot, a large, blue-bedecked beast with a fierce horn. The Crown Jewels are the cheerleaders on loan from the London Monarchs, the capital's American Football side. They're pretty good, but as the evening gets chilly they look a bit underdressed. There are clowns, there is a barbecue and a crèche, and there is a jolly, if slightly contrived, atmosphere. There is quite a good game at the interval where if you catch a rugby ball thrown into the crowd by a Crown Jewel, you get the chance to have a kick at goal. If you convert the goal you win a new car. The competition is not open to professional sportsmen and tonight's kicker clearly hasn't been practising. In his pair of loafers he misses by a mile.

The Broncos are selling themselves and making a lot of noise. In fact, the Broncos are shouting themselves hoarse. But the game itself is worth the fuss – yes, there is a game in there somewhere – and London Broncos tweak the Rhinos by the horn. It finishes 40–16 after the Broncos had taken a 28–0 lead by the interval. The Broncos' bold new signing is Shaun Edwards, the former icon of Wigan and the man with the tag of the most decorated player in the game. Edwards comes off just after the break with rib damage. You know it is serious when Edwards leaves the field. Here is a player who played in the 1990 Challenge Cup final against Warrington with a depressed fracture of the cheekbone and multiple fractures of the eye socket. He has come to London at the age of 30 to try and blend in with this mix of largely Australian players and play in an alien culture. In Wigan he would have been mobbed. In Richmond High Street he could walk unrecognised. Edwards's former Wigan club-mate Martin Offiah has joined him at The Stoop. The wing is dividing his time between the Broncos and Bedford, an exhausting schedule, and he is not playing for his league paymasters tonight.

Edwards, at 30, has since his arrival been overshadowed by the 25-year-old Sydneysider Josh White, who tonight scores a clever try, one of the Broncos' seven. Their backing-up and passing is impressive. The Broncos look a more cohesive unit than Leeds, and Ronnie looks forlorn as the game slips away from the visitors. One unwelcome aspect to the game, though, is the influence of the giant screen at the end which holds the disconsolate huddle of Leeds supporters. The referee asks for an action replay when he suspects one of Broncos' second-half tries, by their wing Scott Roskell, to have been scored from a forward pass. It was not and the try is allowed, but surely the referee should make an instant decision, albeit perhaps a flawed one, rather than rely on an action replay? Here is another innovation that alienates the paying customer.

As the crowd file away and the Tannoy urges them to stay and drink in the bars afterwards, the press are invited to interview any of the players and the Broncos' Australian coach Tony Currie in the dressing-room. The Broncos are nothing if not accessible. This is a slightly surreal experience, for there on the individually marked Harlequins' seats in the dressing-rooms sit the Broncos players in various states of undress. On the seats marked 'Will Carling', 'Jason Leonard' and even 'Steve Pilgrim' sit Peter Gill, Tulsen Tollett and David Krause, while Josh White skips about in his underpants and Shaun Edwards and Martin Offiah chat quietly in the corner. Currie talks affably about his side's chances in the Super League. 'Take us as you find us' is the Broncos' attitude. There is no front to this side.

Two years earlier, all this would have been unimaginable. In the inner sanctum of Harlequins, a bunch of matey Australian rugby league players swigging lager and joking with members of the press. What would Adrian Stoop have made of it all? And how did this sport, once confined to the banks of the Humber and the Mersey, find itself in the swim by the Thames? In two words, Super League. During the 1995–96 season Rupert

Murdoch plunged £87 million into the development of Super League in a long-term agreement that included broadcasting rights for his Sky television. Super League began in the spring of 1996 and rugby league became a summer sport. No longer competing with union, it broke out of its entrenched northern shell to exist alongside the winter game of union. It was brasher, bolder and with its new-found wealth more vulgar. But Murdoch's Super League could not have existed without the Brisbane Broncos. The Broncos made a downbeat start in the 1988 Australian Rugby League Premiership but their owners Barry Maranta and Paul Morgan had big ideas. They used a marketing strategy aimed at women and families to entice them to watch games. Within five years they had won the Australian Rugby League Premiership and crowds of 40,000 were watching them.

In 1994 Barry Maranta, a former history lecturer who went on to sell real estate, bought the London Crusaders and renamed them the Broncos. His son Michael joined the club as a shareholder the following year. The three-year deal with Harlequins, Maranta says, means they are 'no longer the London Gypsies'. Speaking in one of the Broncos' hospitality lounges in The Stoop's East Stand following the defeat of Leeds, Barry Maranta is a happy man. Above us is the ubiquitous television screen which is showing a gridiron match from the World Bowl. 'See that?' he says. 'That game is also about merchandising.'

Maranta says he has been a 'voyeur of American sport for 20 years'. The Brisbane Broncos were named after the Denver Broncos. His true passion, he says, is cricket, claiming that cricket and rugby league have been the most myopic of sports in the past. But, he says, 'You don't sell anything unless it is a good product. Eighteen months ago we were getting crowds of 800. At Charlton we were getting 5,000. Now we're getting an average of 6,000. But we won't wake up one morning and discover 20,000 are coming to watch us. We have to work on the playing side and work to establish a rugby culture down here. We sacked a lot of players last year because they weren't good enough, but apart from Martin Offiah and Shaun Edwards we aren't buying scrapbooks. We're buying potential and that is more exciting.

You have a choice. You can either buy scrapbooks like Sir John Hall has done or buy rawer material. And we are not stupidly buying a team.'

Maranta has lost heavily in his first three years in Britain but says that the Broncos will eventually make a profit. Richard Branson has also invested a 15 per cent stake in the club. Maranta junior's task is to find more City backing for the Broncos. 'Instead of being the poor relations of Harlequins we can play an important part in the strategic planning at a club that has already seen what our game can offer through the skills of Gary Connolly and Robbie Paul during the union season. With big business people coming into the game, people like Sir John Hall, Nigel Wray and Richard Branson, here the future looks good.'

Maranta senior admits that persuading local newspapers and local radio stations to plug his venture has been difficult, and there are lots of gripes in the Broncos' fanzine *London Calling* about this perceived lack of coverage in London's *Evening Standard*. There are 5,919 at the Leeds game, which is more than the average crowd at Harlequins, yet rugby league has perhaps a quarter of the coverage rugby union receives in the national press. Rugby league's real problem in the South, though, is developing local players. The Rugby Football League has funded development posts and Bev Risman, the former Great Britain captain and team manager of Fulham RLFC in the late '80s, is now the director of development at the Broncos, trying to promote the game at local schools.

But the real unanswered question about the new links between rugby league and rugby union is not whether Shaun Edwards takes Will Carling's clothes peg in the Quins dressing-room. It is whether Rupert Murdoch's money in Super League and now rugby union will lead to one code. Ask Barry Maranta this and he just says gnomically, 'I could never have imagined us playing at Harlequins or Gary Connolly and Robbie Paul coming here. My imagination is just not that elastic. Now I look at rugby union and see the breakaway forwards and ask, "Why do we need 15 players?" Okay, when they were smaller and slower. But do we need them now?' His question is left hanging in the air.

I like Barry Maranta. He is alarmingly up front and can-do in a typically Australian way. What rugby union administrator would buy a total stranger a drink and 15 minutes later give him his home telephone number and tell him to give him a call if he wanted to know anything else? And I like the Broncos. But it will be a problem for them to sell their game to sceptical folk like me in the South. Rugby union and rugby league are fine sports, but about as similar as cricket and baseball. I don't want to deny people their pleasures, whether they are completely baffling to me, like trainspotting or sumo wrestling, or just not quite my cup of tea, like rugby league. Rugby league is tremendously athletic, there is fingertip passing and uncompromising tackling, and the ball is in play for almost all the match. There is a raw excitement, but, for me, there are too many tries and too little in the way of organised defence to pierce.

It is all a question of taste. Many people asked me during the 1996–97 season if I had seen the Super-12 games and weren't they just fantastic? Well, Wellington 60, Otago 34 may have been the best game ever and everyone has to admire the athleticism and power of the Southern Hemisphere game. But my idea of fun is not necessarily watching a succession of 16 tries and 80 minutes of frenetic, lung-bursting action, all watched over by an indulgent referee who dare not spoil the fun by once blowing his whistle for irritating little things like an offside or a knock-on. Many people may have thought the 1995 World Cup final, where there were no tries in a match that went into extra-time, was a trifle dull, but I found it compelling. Great defence and a real sense of drama. Similarly, Wasps won the first Courage League title of the professional era with some brick-wall defence. Leicester's Joel Stransky, the man whose drop-goal broke the World Cup final deadlock, said that Wasps' defence was so good you almost gave up trying to score tries against them.

A well-drilled rolling maul can be as difficult a facet of the game to play properly as a sparkling three-quarter move. And it is the tries that break the deadlock of these close encounters that remain in the memory more often than those lost in a welter of other tries. The special bits of skill that unlock a tight defence, that little bit of legerdemain, that explosive break or reverse pass, those bits of cool thinking in the midst of the muddy mayhem . . . those are the skills that I would pay to watch rather than be paid to watch. Jeremy Guscott has those skills, as does Gregor Townsend. They are the cool-headed safe-breakers – but they would not necessarily prosper in the starker, crueller game of rugby league.

The Broncos should be welcome in the capital because they are helping break down a century of antipathy between the two codes. They are not quite the first frontiersmen of rugby league in the deep South, though. In 1965 the London Amateur Rugby League was founded by a bunch of Northerners at the rather unlikely setting of Hackney Conservative Club, and its first matches were played on Hackney Marshes. The London League's teams now play the game from venues as far east as Ipswich and as far south as Basingstoke. For years they have actually shared grounds, and sometimes players, with union clubs, with Twickenham turning a blind eye or not seeing at all. Wasps' old ground at Sudbury actually hosted the finals of the London League before the wall came down in 1995.

I am pleased to say that in my own minute way I, too, had a part to play in this coming together of the two codes in the capital. When on the sports desk at the *South London Press* in the early '80s and recording the deeds of the likes of Streatham and Croydon, Old Alleynians and Blackheath – who had a promising No. 8 called Mickey Skinner – I regularly used to hear of Streatham and Croydon players turning out to play rugby league for Peckham or some such club the following day. And I never felt the urge to inform Twickenham. It was the first and last time I have suppressed a hot news story, so I think Barry Maranta owed me that drink.

CHAPTER FOURTEEN

The Whistle-Blower

Back in the mists of time when I was at school, a teacher gave us a lesson on referees. The teacher, Keith Hatter, was a craggy figure who at the time played on the wing at Moseley. 'Referees never make mistakes,' he told his sceptical audience. 'But, sir, they're only human. They must make mistakes,' I said. 'No. They never make mistakes. The referee's decision is always right,' replied Hatter, as if repeating some mantra. Well, 'Sir' was a lot bigger than us so we gave up arguing, but many of his pupils were unconvinced. That theory of refereeing infallibility, though, I found quite comforting over the years. Life changed but referees were always there, like the Pope and the Queen, saying and doing the right things.

Then, at the end of the Pilkington Cup final in 1996, Neil Back shoved the referee Steve Lander, sending him tumbling into a maul of Leicester and Bath players, and was promptly banned for six months. The flanker missed the first quarter of the first professional season and seemed contrite enough, but the portents were not good. Was this what professionalism meant? Assaults on referees, the infallible arbiters, at moments when passions were high or when games had been lost? There had been an earlier high-profile confrontation involving a referee at the end of a match. After England's torrid win in Paris during the quarter-final of the 1991 World Cup, the France coach Daniel Dubroca let fly a volley of abuse at the New Zealand referee David Bishop in the tunnel at Parc des Princes. Dubroca denied an assault on Bishop but was subsequently sacked. Both incidents left a sour taste in the mouth and begged the question of whether referees, without whom there could be no match, were exposed in games where tempers were hot and stakes were high.

The man in the middle, the man in black, the whistle-blower, whatever you call him, or her – and it is often far from flattering – is the 31st and often most important character in the game. The good referee, it is said, is one nobody notices, but with the dawning of the professional era you couldn't help noticing them. The Lander incident, worrying though it might have been at the time, was a trifling one compared to the case of Ben Smoldon, a 19-year-old prop forward condemned to a life in a wheelchair after a rugby injury. The incident resulted in a referee being the key character in a court case in which a QC warned of imminent disaster in the world of rugby union.

Ben Smoldon was playing in the front row for Sutton Coldfield Colts against Burton-on-Trent when a scrum collapsed and he was left with spinal injuries. The referee Michael Nolan, an Army cadet force administrator, had, according to Mr Justice Curtis, failed to take a tight enough grip on the scrums from the start of the game. In the Court of Appeal, Michael Nolan's QC Richard Davies said that amateur referees and schoolteachers would not find turning out on Saturday afternoons too attractive if this was the sort of risk they were going to run. Ben Smoldon had claimed £1 million worth of damages for injuries, and although first-class referees are insured against such incidents and judges stressed that the case did not relate to senior and international games, the Smoldon case set alarm bells ringing for referees. There were fears that refereeing such a physical and highly charged contact sport had become too risky in terms of insurance requirements and perhaps the Lander incident and the Smoldon case would drive more and more potential men in the middle to the golf course or the DIY centre on Saturday afternoons.

During the 1996–97 season Steve Griffiths was the referees' national development officer at the RFU's Centre of Excellence at

Castlecroft in the West Midlands. Griffiths doesn't believe that refereeing has become more hazardous than in the amateur days. 'Most of the guys have grown up in a competitive environment and are used to highly charged games,' he says. 'But what they are noticing is the change in pace of matches and, at the top level, the change in nationality of the players. But the decision-making processes are exactly the same. You make intuitive, instinctive decisions. And if you are starting to worry about them because the game is professional, then it's time to pack it in.'

Twickenham has devised a number of programmes to train referees, from Pilkington level one, for officials of Under-seven to Under-12 level, through teachers' certificates, club certificates and a nationally graded foundation programme to an RFU panel for referees who cover the top four leagues. When the game went professional, the RFU Commission worked out a pay scale for referees. In League One during the 1996–97 season the men in the middle were paid £200 a game, in League Two £150, in League Three £100 and in League Four £75. For a Five Nations match the pay would be a handsome £1,500.

For that money the referee risks an afternoon of smart-alec abuse from a crowd, vilification in the press and constant back-chat from players, all topped off with being pinned to some clubhouse bar by some beery bore who swears that the try you gave against his side resulted from a forward pass three minutes earlier. It doesn't sound like a great alternative to an afternoon on the golf course, but Ed Morrison loves it. At 45, Morrison, a former fly-half with Bristol Harlequins and a player who had no pretensions of gracing Twickenham with his skills, has graced the rugby fields of the world with his matey but firm refereeing. With his neat grey hair and weather-beaten complexion, the trim, smartly turned-out figure is our most recognisable referee. In arguably the grandest and most famous game of all, the 1995 World Cup final between South Africa and New Zealand in Johannesburg, who should be in the picture as Joel Stransky is lining up his winning drop-goal, a kick a whole nation drew its breath for and blew over the crossbar, but Ed Morrison. He is like the character in the Woody Allen film *Zelig*: always in the picture at key moments in history. Part of the action but not part of the action.

'Have a chip, ref. It's a bribe. We've got to win today.' The banter is light-hearted as Ed Morrison walks past the clubhouse at Heywood Road. The chips are down. Sale are playing Leicester in the final game of the 1996–97 season with a place in Europe at stake. The following day Morrison is refereeing at the Henley Sevens, an event which won't make the headlines and which will go unnoticed by 98 per cent of the country's rugby following. But Sale versus Leicester is a landmark fixture of the season. Not life and death but more important than that, as the old joke goes. The national press, critical pens poised, and, more importantly, the all-seeing eye of television are there to blow the whistle on the whistle-blower.

Morrison agrees with Steve Griffiths that it is vital not to dwell too much on the implications of decisions in important matches but to act instinctively and to treat every game the same, whether it's Wales versus England or a game between prep schools. Professionalism, he says, has not made his job less enjoyable or more fractious. But, he says, 'There's no doubt that the game has changed dramatically because so much rests on each match. There are not too many matches where the result is not all-important. You have to bear in mind that players are under contract and win bonuses are at stake and that this can have a bearing on their attitudes.

'I'm friendly with a top soccer referee and he said to me in the summer before this season started that we had to prepare for some big changes. He basically said "Watch this space". But one of the most pleasing aspects for me is the fact that, so far, our relationship with the players hasn't changed. Of course we have our off-days when players don't like this decision or don't like that, but that's refereeing. But I think that if we're going to go forward, then the referees, players and coaches have to go forward collectively. I've been very pleased this season to see players with a smile on their face, because although it may be their job and is still obviously important to them, I think we can still enjoy what we do.'

To keep pace with the modern game Morrison trains three times a week in a Bristol gym. He runs and does aerobic sessions. 'When you have players training all day to improve their fitness, it is incumbent on all referees to try and keep pace with that change. That doesn't mean that an old man like me can be as fit as a 22-year-old, but you've got to be seen to be trying to bridge that gap. Every referee I know takes great personal pride in his fitness. One of the reasons why we can live with the faster game is that we're working much harder ourselves and putting more time into training. All the younger refs are doing weight-training now. I think it's a bit too late for me to try and put that power on. As part of training, all referees need to look to explore every avenue they can to improve their level of fitness and performance. The last thing any of us wants to do is to make ourselves look more foolish than we already do.'

Like many referees, Morrison is a former player who got injured but who loved the game so much he could never watch from the sidelines. 'I got this knee injury and was told to stop playing. I was 25 but unfortunately I didn't take any notice of the surgeon – which was to my cost, because I broke every bone going after that. I eventually gave up at 32. I used to work as an engineer for British Aerospace but before the World Cup in 1995 I had a difficult decision to make. I was spending so much time away from work and the company was going through a reorganisation period and a lot of people were losing their jobs. Well, I was going off to South Africa for six weeks that year and all around me people were being asked to empty their desks and it just became impossible. So I left in the January, started my own sports consultancy and never looked back.

'What I have seen from my experiences in the Southern Hemisphere is that they are five or ten years ahead of us in respect of this word "professionalism". It was a word you heard whispered in the North, but they accepted that if the game was to move forward then you had to spend more time on improving your skills and your fitness. I'm absolutely delighted that the decision was made in Paris. It ignited the game. Contrary to what some people think, it was just being totally unrealistic to expect the players to carry on as they were. At the end of the day we should always consider the players. I'm old-fashioned enough to think that the game is about the players. People don't come to watch me, they come to watch the likes of Jeremy Guscott, and I think we should always be talking about the playing side of the game rather than anything else. But the reality was that the demands on the players were totally unacceptable. Unless you were lucky enough to have an employer who was totally sympathetic to the game of rugby, there was no way you could compete at international level. When you look back, the real sponsors of English rugby were the employers of the players who enabled them to have the time to improve their skills.'

So far Morrison has thankfully not found that the prediction of his soccer refereeing friend has been proved true – namely, that a professional game is less fun and that the referee has to watch his back and scoot off home as soon as, as Bill McLaren so singularly puts it, 'the referee's whistle blows for no side'. 'You have to be aware of what is riding on the game. It would be disrespectful if you didn't. But at the end of the day I'm a simple soul and my attitude to any game that I ref is to go out and give it my best. You can relate refereeing to playing. No player goes out to make mistakes but the reality is that we all do make them. The important thing is not to try to fool the players or the spectators and to own up when you have made them. And once the game is over the ref is still treated like a guest at the club.

'I still feel like a guest and some of the clubs are magnificent. At Kingsholm, performing in front of the Shed may be tricky, but the club is still fantastically hospitable. If I bring friends or members of my family along, they are treated like royalty. Leicester and Northampton are the same. The clubs are still fantastically warm places. If you've given a penalty against them, they tell you they're disappointed but they'll buy you a beer and talk about it. If you have had a difficult game it's still important to make your presence felt in the bar afterwards and face the players. I'm in the game purely and simply because I enjoy it. I'm no different from anyone else. I've got a family. They don't particularly want to read about me making myself look a right plonker but the game is a way of life and this season I've enjoyed it more than ever. Saturdays to me are rugby days where you learn as much off the pitch as on the pitch.'

Morrison does think, though, that players need a greater understanding of the laws of the game. 'It's a very complex sport and it's crazy to think that here we are trying to play a game that nobody understands all the laws of. There's no other sport in the world where players are so unsure of those laws. But things have improved dramatically over the last few years. When I first started at first-class level there were some players like Brian Moore, Paul Turner and Gary Rees who had a deep understanding of the laws, but they were the exception. I always said Gary Rees would make a very good referee. Knowing the laws helps them understand the game and I think that's something we need to work on. The major rule changes over the last few years have made rugby a different game. They have speeded the game up and made it much more enjoyable from the spectator's point of view. I don't think any other sport would have been brave enough or naive enough to have made the number of law changes that rugby has, but a few years ago we were all beginning to wonder where the game was going. We were having balls stuffed up the jumper, nobody could see the ball and it was difficult for the spectator to get involved.'

But even the ever-cheery Ed Morrison sees future problems in recruiting enough high-quality referees. Referees now have public liability insurance of up to £5 million. But, as Morrison says, 'There was a lot of emotion about the Smoldon case and in my club, where we don't have a full-time referee, this guy who would referee told me not to ask him again. If there was no insurance the game would disintegrate and the reality already is that there are fewer people who are prepared to referee. There are two reasons for that. I think society is changing and it has almost become a ritual to abuse the referee. We have learned that from soccer. He's "the bastard in the black" and all that nonsense. That is a problem, because some people naturally are offended if they have to put up with abuse and aren't getting paid a penny for what they do. The other problem is that someone may decide that refereeing sounds an attractive thing to do but after a time he discovers that he aspires to a level he isn't going to reach and then he leaves the game, spending Saturday afternoons going shopping with the wife or playing golf. There are so many alternative things to do in your leisure time nowadays that these characters, the lifeblood of the game, just disappear.'

And so the Sale versus Leicester match kicks off. The man in black is a man in yellow today, in a match of unrelenting ferocity. Morrison has a difficult time keeping the lid on a game that often steams over into violent confrontation. There are five punch-ups, the worst between Leicester's scrum-half Austin Healey and the Sale hooker Steve Diamond, and Morrison has to lecture both captains, Martin Johnson, who is involved in a free-for-all himself, and Sale's Jim Mallinder. And controversy is not far away. After the 20–20 draw which gives Leicester their place in the European sun, the Sale camp complain about the lack of injury-time despite there having been a long stoppage for treatment to their lock Dave Erskine. There is also the inevitable penalty-try which ultimately robs Sale of their deserved two points.

At the start of the final quarter the Leicester pack rumbles forward and forces five scrums close to the Sale line. Morrison warns the Sale pack for twice bringing down the scrum and awards the penalty try when it happens a third time. But even that all-seeing eye of television fails to confirm the decision. Yes, the scrum collapsed, but would the Sale pack collapse it deliberately when the outcome is to concede seven points? The penalty try was once a rare affliction but we saw a flood of them in the 1996–97 season and in these circumstances the defending side always sees itself wronged.

The game ends in a storm of booing. It has been so nerve-racking and bitter that even Leicester's Tiger mascot, a 52-year-old HGV driver in a stripy nylon suit, almost comes to blows on the pitch with two youngsters who try to rugby-tackle him. The Henley Sevens will seem like an oasis of calm for Ed Morrison after all this. But true to his word, there he is in the Heywood Road bar after the match, enjoying a beer or three with all of us one-eyed critics. And, at that moment, as Saracens are finishing their roller-coaster of a season with an unexpected victory over Bath at Enfield, their fez-wearing supporters are breaking out into another chorus of ritualised abuse: 'He's blind, he's deaf, he wants to be a ref.' There must be easier ways of earning £200.

CHAPTER FIFTEEN

The Making of a Will

There are some, it seems, who are born to be rugby players. Thus A. Forward, who played in Wales's back row in their 1952 Grand Slam team, was destined for a place in a pack somewhere, just as Dodge, Trick, Hare and Swift were aptly named England backs of the '80s. And how could someone called Austin Healey ever be a slouch, or W.E. Bastard, a Springbok in the '30s, be anything other than a, well, an awkward opponent?

Will Greenwood seems to have come from some rugby-player mould. The son of the former England captain and coach Richard, Greenwood, the strapping Leicester centre, is also from the same Sedbergh School and Durham University stable as that other Will, Carling. His initials could well be those inscribed ironically by Mike Atherton's Lancashire team-mates on his cricket bag: FEC, or Future England Captain. 'I can remember my second birthday. I got a cricket bat, a pair of boxing gloves and one of those old-fashioned brown rugby balls,' he says. And he has been running with the ball ever since.

Greenwood senior once memorably said, 'The amateur rugby union player has an inalienable right to play like a pillock.' This dictum was quite a useful way to explain away a poor performance in the old days. 'Well, I was putting up the MFI

146

furniture this morning and I did my back in' or 'We've been a bit short-handed on the old farm this week' were useful stand-bys.

There is no hiding-place, though, for Greenwood junior, who in his first season with Leicester was not good enough for England but was good enough for the Lions. He is a professional but, when we meet, he is suffering from something money can't protect amateur or professional sportsmen from, namely painful injury. It is the most vital fortnight of Leicester's season. In two days' time they travel to Sale for a final league game in which the winners take the final English berth in the following season's European Cup. A week later the sides meet again in the Pilkington Cup final. There is no money at stake for the club but it is their only hope of silverware in a season in which they were overtaken by Wasps in the league and trounced in the European Cup final by France's Brive.

In Leicester's centre during the 1996–97 season the letter 'M' on Will Greenwood's back might have stood for 'Majestic', as his sharp running, good handling and crunching tackling helped give the Tigers some midfield bite. Leicester, often fairly, have had a reputation in recent years for playing a ten-man game which, while effective, has been less than enthralling to watch. But the key signings at the beginning of the season of Greenwood, who had struggled to hold down a regular place for Harlequins, and Healey, the Orrell scrum-half, helped add a new dimension to Leicester's game. Healey is the quickest scrum-half in the land, a converted wing whose speed, combined with the new laws preventing back rows from leaving a scrum until the ball has cleared it, helps him create panic in opposition defences.

But Greenwood has been the most improved English player of the 1996–97 season. The strength in his 6ft 4in, 14 stone frame enables him to stand up in tackles and gain that extra yard or two, and he has footballing nous. In the cup semi-final it was his perfectly weighted bobbing kick just before he was enveloped by a Gloucester tackler that enabled Steve Hackney to sprint away for the winning try. Earlier in the season Healey had scored a breathtaking try in a European Cup game against Llanelli, but it was Greenwood's basketball pass under pressure that had created the vital breakthrough and a try for Leon Lloyd.

'Greenwood has midfield awareness when he's under pressure. This quality will come out on the Lions tour,' the Lions coach Ian McGeechan predicted on the day the tour party was announced. 'I think he can do for us what Scott Gibbs did in 1993 and what Jeremy Guscott did in 1989.' Greenwood has enjoyed receiving the plaudits, but now that M could stand for 'Moody'. Being selected as only the seventh uncapped player since the war to play for the Lions is all very well, but an ankle damaged against Wasps earlier in April had cut his season short. He came back ten days later, but damaged ligaments caused him to hobble off in the second half against Bath. We are sitting in the back garden of the house he rents with Healey and the Scottish wing Craig Joiner in the Leicestershire village of Botcheston, the sun is shining, the birds are singing, voters in the village hall across the road are helping change the course of political history – but that ankle is painful. Three weeks of physio and hanging around are taking their toll.

'What's being a professional like? That's a question we get asked a hundred times. Professionalism is good. It allows you rest and recuperation, the chance to learn about nutrition. It basically allows you to perform to the best of your ability every Saturday. The problem is midweek games, but if you have the normal week's rest you can play back-to-back Saturdays. Having a full-time job as well is very difficult. But injuries are the big problem. You do get very bored. You end up hanging around the rugby club. Because you get half an hour's treatment every day you're not really using up all your energy, so you find yourself struggling to know what to do. But the other side of the coin is that you get better quicker because you get more treatment and because you allow your body to recover. Most of the leading players are going away for tours and the next season looks quite punishing for them, with it beginning on 23 August and the games being virtually back to back until 5 May.'

The new, ultra-competitive game has brought its problems even to clubs with strong squads like Leicester. During April 1997 they were forced to play five games in 15 days. In one week, containing a Tuesday-night defeat at Gloucester four days before the thrashing at Bath when Leicester were out on their feet for the final quarter, the Tigers' championship hopes were brought to an end and alarm was triggered in the top end of the game. 'Leicester's five games in two weeks shouldn't be allowed to happen because of the physical nature of rugby. We would have fought tooth and nail to stop that congestion. That kind of fixture log-jam is dangerous in a game of rugby,' said the Bath coach Andy Robinson.

The sheer physical demands of the sport along with boredom may be the downside of professionalism, but players like Greenwood and Healey, both with recently won degrees have qualifications and careers to fall back on should injuries cut short their present careers. Turning professional was not an automatic decision even for someone like Will Greenwood, though. He had a lucrative career in a City merchant bank and he admits he misses it. 'I had done a year and a half working for five days in the City and playing for Quins at the same time. I'm not a great mornings man and I was getting up at quarter to six every morning for five days. Tuesdays and Thursdays were training nights and the only way I could get to training was to take my kit-bag to work and go to Quins straight afterwards. To do my own fitness routines I would work in the gym on Mondays and Wednesdays. I never had lunch. I would just have that at my desk, so all my personal training had to be after work. We travelled together on Fridays and games were on Saturdays, so I found that too much was being compressed into too short a space of time. Getting up at quarter to six and getting home at ten o'clock Monday to Friday just took its toll. I thought after a while, "I'm not too keen on this." Then I approached the company if I could do a three-day week. They said that was fine. Suddenly life was a lot rosier. I would leave the office on Friday and not be back until the next Wednesday. I could relax on Sundays and Mondays and get some training done on Tuesdays. The routine allowed me to play and work.

'Then, after a Barbarians match in Dublin, I had a chat with Rory Underwood and he asked me if I would fancy coming to Leicester. I said I would think about it. At Quins at the time I was never an automatic choice. If Carling was fit or back from England it was a case of Peter Mensah or myself being left out of the side. Most of the time it was me who didn't play. With European rugby starting, I thought I needed first-team rugby. I didn't particularly want to leave London because I had a lot of good mates there and enjoyed working, but if I had stayed there I would have liked to have continued working but that wouldn't have fitted in with Harlequins' plans. They're now going full-blast with professionalism, having only full-time players. If I had stayed in London I wouldn't have wanted to hang around and just be a rugby player. I decided that by continuing to work and play I wasn't giving my best in either. I wasn't giving 100 per cent, so I thought, well, I don't want to be a sad loser at 32 saying that maybe, just maybe, I could have played for England. But I'll probably be a sad loser anyway.'

This seems unlikely for the 24-year-old who captained the A side so successfully during the 1996–97 season. Will Carling's international retirement and the need to look beyond Jeremy Guscott for the 1999 World Cup would surely hasten opportunities for young Turks like Greenwood, Nick Greenstock of Wasps and Sale's Jos Baxendell to take their spin in the heavy midfield traffic. All these young players are adding to the strength of a First Division which is harder and faster. 'People say it's becoming faster,' says Will Greenwood. 'But the change has been gradual. It's like growing up with an older brother. People say he's getting bigger but you don't notice because you're growing up with him. Being with the professional game from day one has been the same. The influx of foreign players has annoyed a lot of people. It hasn't annoyed me but it could be dangerous to the home game if the right balance isn't found. The game in England will get better and people will learn from them but there will be fewer opportunities for young lads, although you need a squad system as the fixture-list grows.

'I don't think crowds are less forgiving now that we are professionals. I think crowds always criticise if you're not doing well. People have just noticed the harsher criticism now and are willing to put the blame for that at the door of professionalism. If you play badly the crowd is always going to get on your back. I think what we're noticing now is that there is a pressure on you to perform and the consequences are greater now that it is your job. If you are not doing work well for your employer you get sacked.

'We have the game to qualify for Europe this weekend. It's like getting a promotion or a pay rise at work if you can get into Europe. If you don't get into Europe you don't give yourself the platform on which to perform. What games will you get picked for England on? You'll get picked on your displays in a European Cup final or semi-final. You might not get picked for England if you do well in an Anglo-Welsh game. You need the big games to put your case forward. That's why many of the players are moving to top clubs, to play with the best players and to improve by playing at that higher level. But it puts unnecessary pressure on some players. I'm not saying this because I'm injured, but when you are injured the managers and coaches want you on the pitch because they realise the vast importance of each result. Now and then you think, this is all well and good, but someone should be looking after the welfare of the players who are performing on the Saturdays, otherwise you will see a lot of burn-out.'

Behind us in the haze of the afternoon sunshine, Austin Healey and his girlfriend throw a rugby ball to and fro. It eventually lands in the field behind the house. Will Greenwood eyes them enviously, rubs his sore ankle and yawns. Muscles bulging out of his T-shirt but nobody to play with. A caged Tiger.

Will Greenwood failed to recover for that weekend's trip to Sale. The match marks the end of the first season of professional league rugby union in England and it encapsulates everything that is good and bad in the modern game, every contradiction and every quirk that has made the season so fascinating. The match had earlier been billed as a dress rehearsal for the Pilkington Cup final a week later, but it turns out to be a compelling drama in its own right. It finishes 20–20 with a late penalty from Joel Stransky saving a point for Leicester and ensuring them the fourth place in the European Cup the following season at Sale's expense. And expense is the word. Sale, by the end of the season, were some half a million pounds in debt. A European venture would have helped them cancel out those debts.

The match is fractious, bitter, fast and furious. And yet Sale's tiny Heywood Road ground in the southern suburbs of Manchester and on the wealthy borders of Cheshire is not even full for their most important game of the season. A temporary stand at one end has more wide, open spaces than the pitch. There are barely 5,000 souls to witness the spectacle. On another side of Manchester twice that many watch Bury defeat Millwall in a Second Division soccer match that receives a fraction of the coverage in the national press. The Heywood Road ground is typical of countless rugby clubs. It is cramped and cosy, the spectators spill outside the clubhouse with their pints, the smell of hot dogs and hamburgers fills the air, and there is a raffle for cup-final tickets and a general mood of boozy *bonhomie*. An essentially changeless picture of Middle England.

But Heywood Road, for all its charm and friendliness, is inadequate for top-quality rugby. On the pitch, that rugby transcends its surroundings. It is unyielding, deadly serious and everything is at stake. But for all that both clubs have invested in full-time players, the key man, Will Greenwood, is missing. He has to watch while Jim Mallinder, a PE teacher at Manchester's William Hulme School, slices through the Leicester defence time and again. Mallinder is the best player on the pitch, yet he is still essentially an amateur. He would probably relish the opportunity to be as bored as Will Greenwood. His schedule has been punishing, sometimes meeting at the club at seven in the morning to train before driving off to school, then after school returning to Heywood Road for team sessions. The school has given him Fridays off for travelling to away matches. It is clearly too punishing a routine, and at the end of the season Mallinder, chosen for England's tour to Argentina, elects to become a professional at the age of 31.

And more contradictions. Sale may be characterised as the homely northern outpost of the sport but they have moved swiftly into the professional era. Two of their key players in the 1996–97 season were New Zealanders, the former Waikato flanker John Mitchell, who was outstanding in the back row and whose role as player-coach made him arguably the wisest import in the English game, and the All Black fly-half Simon Mannix, an astute kicker and playmaker. And at the end of the week Sale announce a £2.5 million backer who can help the club keep pace with the top sides in the land.

Sale's stock on the field may have risen throughout the 1996–97 season, but cold cash is still needed to keep sides together. On the last Saturday of the league season, though, there are still more important things than winning and losing. One of Sale's prop forwards, Mark Ridehalgh, has been forced to give up the game at the age of 30 after lesions were discovered on his brain, and buckets are passed around to raise money. The front row will always be a dangerous place to earn a living.

CHAPTER SIXTEEN

Stranded on the Hard Shoulder

Dave Whelan, the multi-millionaire who owns the Wigan Athletic soccer club, was asked after the team's promotion to the Second Division had been assured just how much he may have to help Wigan gain promotion to the First the following year. He thought for a while before casually replying, 'Oh, about £30 million.' Whelan, a former Blackburn Rovers player, is head of JJB, the stores group specialising in replica football kits, and by the end of 1997 the group had about 220 shops in high streets and superstores. At the start of the year total sales were over £130 million. Money can't buy you everything, as Whelan discovered when he made an unsuccessful attempt to take over Wigan Warriors rugby league club. But it helps. Across town at Orrell they could do with some of the loose change from a few of Dave Whelan's shops. Orrell were the village club that survived cheek-by-jowl with the best town clubs in the land for a decade. But with the advent of the big City backers and the asset strippers, Orrell RUFC (1996) found itself swimming against the financial tide.

It is 26 April 1997, the cricket season has begun and the grey skies of Wigan are naturally weeping buckets of rain. There have been plenty of rainy days this season for Orrell. Today is Orrell's

73rd game in the First Division and it is their last. In a decade, Orrell have won 42 of those games at their tiny Edge Hall Road ground. Every one of the more fashionable clubs has lost there. But not this season. This season only West Hartlepool, to be relegated along with Orrell, and London Irish have lost in the suburbs of Wigan, and away from home Orrell have won only a single match, a last defiant victory at London Irish. Orrell finish rooted firmly at the foot of the table, having conceded 886 points. Theirs is a tale of the haves and have-nots, of North versus South. Orrell are the victims of a professional game – but they may yet prosper.

For students of trivia, Orrell actually played the first game of the professional season in England. Because of the presence of Sky TV cameras for their opening game against the champions Bath, the match at Edge Hall Road kicked off early in front of a shirt-sleeved crowd at the end of August. There was the usual optimism from Orrell and talk in the programme about once more 'making the prophets of doom eat their words'. The picture on the front of the programme was of Frano Botica, the former All Black who had switched codes to play gloriously across town at Wigan. Lately at Castleford, Botica had moved to Edge Hall Road in the summer. It was hoped his consummate skills as a playmaking fly-half who could kick goals in his sleep would galvanise the callow Orrell backs. Worryingly for Orrell, they had lost 18 players in the summer. Simon Mason, the Ireland full-back who had been raised on the Wirral, took up a lucrative contract at Richmond, and Austin Healey had walked out on the club before the end of the previous season to pursue a successful career at Leicester. Within 12 months Healey, the turbo-charged scrum-half, had won a place in the Lions squad and his move seemed logical. More worryingly for Orrell, though, was that many members of the bright young side who had played such exhilarating rugby in the last amateur season had moved on to clubs like Waterloo, Wakefield and Leeds. Even League Two clubs, they felt, could offer them better career prospects and better wage packets.

And ominously for Orrell, Richard Webster, the Welsh flanker who had returned to union, was now turning out for Bath instead of Orrell, who thought they had captured the former Lion earlier in the summer but were unable to come close to Bath's market valuation. Des Seabrook, the new Orrell president, former coach of the North and member of the old school, sounded a warning and hinted that putting players under contract was not always a good idea. Thanking everyone for helping at the club, he said, 'But how long will the club member exist as we know him? The numbers in every club are dwindling and with players on lucrative contracts soon everyone will be paid for doing the most menial jobs.'

Edge Hall Road, normally packed to the rafters for this glamorous fixture, was less than three-quarters full. Perhaps Orrell's members were voting with their feet, perhaps they were still on holiday, perhaps they were too engrossed in the summer Super League or cricket season to notice the Courage League's unaccustomed early kick-off. Whatever, Bath, looking like they had spent a considerable time conditioning in the gym during the summer to prepare for the demands of the rigorous professional era, ran Orrell off their feet. Bath won 56–13, scoring six crisply executed tries, and Webster was a revelation. And Bath's director of rugby John Hall was not even pleased with his side. 'Could do better' was the general comment from Bath. Botica, polite but subdued, remarked that the young Orrell side had shown 'plenty of spirit'. There was one consolation for Orrell in the dazzling running skills of their new full-back from West Park, the cropped-haired Rob Hitchmough. 'I didn't know they had signed Christian Cullen,' said John Hall, with one of his rare jokes. But Orrell weren't laughing. They had been used to losing players, through the demands of rugby league and the job market of the prosperous South, but this was something different. And by the end of the season Hitchmough was on Harlequins' shopping list.

'Until now we've been competing on a level playing field. Now we're on the north wall of the Eiger,' said Seabrook. The days of amateur rugby were over, but how could Orrell compete in a professional era without any money? During the 1996–97 season they didn't even have a major sponsor. How could they afford to lose a team each summer and throw in inexperienced players against fully honed professionals? And things got worse. Botica was lured away to Llanelli after only three matches and Orrell spent the season attempting to wrestle for compensation with the Welsh club. Orrell replaced Botica with Matthew McCarthy, a slightly built Welshman with a shrewd football brain but none of Botica's physical presence, and they continued to lose match after match in the league.

It is hard to know what the low point is when you seem to have plumbed the depths already, but for Orrell it was probably the end of the first series of league games before the top sides turned their attentions to the European Cup. Orrell, already decimated by injuries, took their young side to Harlequins in October and were beaten 89–18. They scored the first and last points of the match but in between they conceded 14 tries. Orrell tackled gamely but Keith Wood, Harlequins' Irish hooker, rampaged all over the field, scattering Orrell forwards like nine-pins, and Gary Connolly, Harlequins' temporary recruit from – irony of ironies – Wigan, cut a swath through the Orrell defence. Many of the spectators in Quins' sponsored boxes didn't bother to watch the second half. Champagne rugby loses some of its sparkle when the opposition can't scramble the cash to buy a crate of brown ale. Even that quintessential Quin Nigel Starmer-Smith was shaking his head after the match. Only the most sadistic Quins supporter could have enjoyed it. Orrell's young players trooped hollow-eyed from the pitch. The following week they struggled to beat Dunvant.

The day of the Harlequins defeat coincided with the starkest reminder that we were now in an era of professional versus amateur or, at best, professional versus semi-professional. Newcastle 156, Rugby 5 and Coventry 102, Nottingham 22 were two of the cricket scores in League Two. All this led to a certain amount of gallows humour on the part of the victims. 'We've got a sponsor, Rugby Cement. Perhaps they can build us a wall in front of our try-line,' laughed Roger Large, the Rugby secretary, before their return league fixture with Newcastle. No, he said, they did not expect to win on aggregate. 'Come to write our obituary, lad?' joked one of Orrell's ever-cheery gatemen as I flashed my press card during the season. But there was no trace of self-pity, or resentment that you have sniffed blood.

'So what?' will be the cynical cry. What if Orrell lost their matches? Surely it meant that they were simply not good enough and now, in a more businesslike age, they had been found wanting. Wasn't the whole point of league rugby to constantly sift the teams at the top so the gold nuggets stayed in the pan? And if Orrell were so marvellous, why did all those players leave, some to lesser but more ambitious clubs? Orrell do matter, though, to anyone who cares for the heart and soul of club rugby. They epitomise the family club. Most of the people connected with Orrell are genuinely friendly. Their players are not remote figures at the end of some mobile phone, but approachable characters who mingle in the clubhouse with friends, family and spectators after the match, sharing a pint while toddlers scurry beneath the forest of tree-trunk thighs. Orrell are an unpretentious club in an unpretentious setting.

From the kitchen comes the waft of food on match-days that I now connect in a Proustian way to what happens on the pitch. That smell of chips, barm cakes, curry and the best meat pies on the rugby circuit will forever remind me of Bob Kimmins churning through the Edge Hall Road mud on another rolling maul. Edge Hall Road is not the prettiest plot of real estate in Orrell, let alone the north-west of England, and the drone of traffic on the M6 provides unwelcome muzak. It has a small stand, where the wind and rain always seem to be directed as if by radar, and a small covered terrace opposite that has similarly not changed in decades.

During the dying days of amateurism, Orrell experimented with two games against the best-followed clubs in the land, Bath and Leicester. Towards the end of the 1995–96 season they came to Wigan's home at Central Park and not Edge Hall Road. But it was as if a tightly knit, happy family had moved into some gloomy old pile for a couple of weekends. We rattled around inside Central Park, crowds of barely 2,000 a time – and these swelled by mainly visiting supporters. Many of Orrell's fans stubbornly refused to watch there. 'Search for the Hero Inside Yourself', that upbeat song by M People which had become something of an anthem for rugby leaguers, blared from the speakers in an attempt to lift everybody's spirits. It didn't. The afternoons were awful and, needless to say, Orrell were well beaten in both matches. The stewards were, for the most part, bone-headed and curtly dismissive. One of them told Starmer-Smith to 'fuck off'. The experiment, thank goodness, would never be repeated. Tellingly, Wigan's supporters ignored the events. They were buggered if they were going to pay good money to watch Jeremy Guscott and Rory Underwood.

This was because Wigan is a rugby league town, the biggest rugby league town in the land, and the Wigan of recent years are the finest exponents of that game. This is another problem for Orrell. The blood of Wigan folk runs cherry red and not black and amber. When I reached Wigan for that final game of the year against Saracens, Wigan's evening paper consisted of wall-to-wall rugby league. There was a 12-page colour pull-out on Super League. There were three paragraphs on Orrell. In the pubs of the town that night everyone was watching and talking about Wigan. They were defeated 14–4 at Salford and the shock was palpable in the streets the morning after. 'Why did they let Shaun Edwards go?' was the mantra. 'Losing again. And to Salford. What a shambles.' In the Touch Line bar in Wigan Lane the men and women watch the humiliation on a giant screen. It is Wigan's fourth defeat of the season and the drinkers groan. Around the walls are pictures of Wigan greats of recent vintage, such as Edwards and Connolly, of the previous generation, such as the peerless Billy Boston, and of the fuzzy, monochrome, pre-war days, such as John Sullivan, the Welshman who played full-back for Wigan and in a glittering career scored over 4,500 points. The fact that Orrell, a haven of rugby union in this rugby league heaven, survive has been a minor miracle.

After Orrell lose Botica, their captain Andy Macfarlane also goes. There are isolated successes but the club looks doomed to lose its premier status. In the end, and following the trend of soccer, the manager, or in this case the director of rugby, goes. Mark Ring at West Hartlepool and John Hall at Bath have already bitten the dust. Now Peter Williams leaves, a week before the 40–14 return match at Bath in April, the result that condemns Orrell to relegation. Williams, a former big-kicking but skilled fly-half, played for England during the 1987 World Cup. He left union, disillusioned after being made a scapegoat for England's failings in Australia, and played rugby league for Salford, returning to Orrell, his old club, as a salaried director of rugby in the autumn of 1995. Will Carling once infamously said that Willams had a 'chip on both shoulders', but the worst thing anyone says about him at Orrell, even after his resignation, is 'He were a bit too nice for the job were Peter'.

Having given up the post he had held for 18 months, Peter Williams returned to his former job as a physiotherapist, going from feeling the strain to healing the strains. And he is not hiding. Williams is there on the terraces watching Orrell in the final League One game at Edge Hall Road. 'In the end,' he says before the match, 'I left through frustration. The biggest factor was money. If you compete at the very top nowadays you have to have some. And I also felt the structure of the club was not correct. People are romantic about the club and there is a lot of goodwill out there, which is nice, but the harsh reality is that rugby is a business now. There are a lot of good things about the amateur ethos but you have to be hard-headed. What the club has got to realise is that its major asset is its players. You have to treat them properly and it's not just a question of money. A lot of things can be done better there.'

Williams says the club's structure is designed for the amateur era. 'Orrell were magnificently run in the amateur era. They have strength and that great family feeling, but they have to grasp the nettle of professionalism and go with the flow. There is no point moaning about it, no point having a chip on your shoulder and being morbid. The forwards have been playing well but the backs lack a sense of direction. Losing Botica was a big blow because he was an exceptional goalkicker and a real professional on and off the pitch. That attitude could have rubbed off on others. To be fair to him he could hardly refuse the money Llanelli were offering him. He weighed up the pros and cons but he wanted to secure his future before returning to New Zealand. That's fair enough. I was disappointed at the time but not bitter. It's a cruel world. We had lost 18 players in the summer and we should have tried harder, in hindsight, to keep them. When you lose 18 players you know you are going to struggle. We should have tried harder to keep players like Wynn and Manley because we had the nucleus of a good side. Simon Mason was offered a deal he couldn't refuse by Richmond and, to be fair to Healey, he's been proved right in moving to Leicester because it has helped him in to the England and Lions sides. We couldn't really hold on to those star players.'

Orrell's players were all part-time professionals and Williams agreed one-year contracts with most of the first team before the 1996–97 season began. The average wage was around £8,000 a year with one player on £14,000. The players also drive a fleet of red Nissan cars, which can be seen bumper to bumper in the Edge Hall Road car park on match-days. 'In November 1995 when I started the job I went to the players and told them that their destiny was in their own hands and that everything was geared to what they did on the pitch. I've found it highly amusing to see how clubs are dealing with professionalism. Some of them haven't got a clue what professionalism is all about. Look, some clubs are in trouble because they've given players contracts worth £40,000 or £45,000 and they're not necessarily first-team players. You just don't chuck that sort of money around. If you're in business you don't give someone £40,000 before you see what he or she can offer the company.' And Williams uses his hands to illustrate his point. 'This is professionalism,' he says, with one flat hand two feet above the other. 'And this is the importance of money,' he adds, shortening the gap to six inches. 'Players have got to concentrate on what they do on the pitch and expect criticism now from the people who pay to watch them. When I went to Salford there was one bloke in the crowd who used to rant at me and Adrian Hadley just because we used to play rugby union. We eventually laughed about it, but because we were being paid people would give us a hard time. And if you are not performing in rugby league, you're out and you don't get paid.

'Orrell, to a certain degree, feel they have done it all, but success is graded in terms of what you win, and they haven't really won anything. I don't know an area where so much rugby is played. There is a real rugby culture here. But Orrell have to compete with Wigan for their support. Wigan are the best rugby league side of the last ten years. People will watch both but the public here is fickle. And Wigan folk do hate Orrell followers. It's infuriating but there it is. When we played those games at Central Park, the father of one of our players refused to come and watch his own son. That's Wigan for you.

'But Orrell will learn by their mistakes. The two props are exceptional, as are Anglesea and Bennett in the back row. They have three-quarters of an exceptionally talented side. The potential is magnificent but has to be realised. At the core Orrell are a strong club and they have the platform for success in the future. The club needs a chief executive and a full-time coach and it may be that the post of director of rugby becomes null and void. I'm firmly of the belief that Orrell need someone from the outside. That's why someone like John Mitchell has done so well at Sale. He had no baggage. He could see what had to be done and he could get on with the job objectively. It didn't matter if he upset a few people along the way. If changes had to be made, they had to be made. Bob Dwyer has had the same sort of effect at Leicester. He may not have been popular at first but he won people over. Now Mitchell has real authority at Sale. I came back and perhaps I was too soft because I knew too many people there and had too many deep feelings for the place. But I've learned a lot in my time there.

'I had a chat with the chairman Ron Pimblett back in January or February and I said I would stay, but there was a lot of unrest by that time and I laid out my theories on what I thought was going wrong. I really believe the club needs to be less insular. When you're not successful, being insular just doesn't help. And when the players think they're not being led properly, this leads to unrest. I'm not decrying the executive. But wouldn't it be worth it if they were to lose power if the club was more successful?'

Williams says there is plenty of raw talent at Orrell. Indeed, in this part of Central Lancashire there is probably the most dense concentration of young players of anywhere in Britain, outside parts of South Wales. Most senior schools play rugby, albeit of two codes. Orrell also have a good relationship with local universities and colleges. One of Orrell's most important figures is Colin Bailey who scouts for student talent. One of his finds, Guy Hope, a young centre from Alsager College, breaks into the first team at the end of the season and scores a smart try in the defeat at Bath. Apart from three sides, a social side and a Colts team, Orrell run Under-17, 16, 15, 14, 13 and 12 teams. The Under-15s have not been beaten for three seasons and the Colts have beaten Newcastle twice.

Already one of those Under-15 players, the centre Richard Welding, has been offered a contract by Wigan. That is something Orrell have had to live with over the years. Williams adds, 'Professionalism is a double-edged sword at Orrell. The world is a bigger oyster for players now with union as well as league clubs hammering at their doors. And I don't want the North to become the feeder area for the South. I look at all these First Division clubs with their northern players and it's depressing, because rugby matters to people up here. I don't want the power to reside in London, the South Midlands and the South-west.'

For Des Seabrook, too, the season has been a chastening one. When I tell him I am going to write a chapter on Orrell, he sounds horrified. 'A chapter? Bloody 'ell.' He feels it may be a bit of a horror story. Seabrook was a Lancashire No. 8 who 25 years earlier helped put Orrell on the map when they defeated Liverpool in the Lancashire Cup final to qualify for the national cup competition. Des Seabrook has for years been the public face of Orrell. A former schoolmaster, he is plain-speaking and tough and does not suffer fools gladly. On the touchlines of northern rugby clubs Des's brown trilby has become as familiar a sartorial symbol as once was Brian Clough's green sweatshirt. Now he wears a rather natty blue felt trilby which he throws on to the desk of his office to make a point. 'When Sir John Hall threw his hat into the ring, he threw a bloody sombrero,' he says. We are sitting in his office next to the Edge Hall Road changing-rooms. The nerve centre of Orrell. Anfield's boot-room must feel like this. Nervous people knock at the door as if it leads to a headmaster's office, and I too feel like I am back at school.

Seabrook admits the club may have been too cautious at the dawning of the new professional age. But he says, 'What most people have forgotten is that at the start of the season there were to have been four relegated clubs from a 12-team First Division. We looked at how other clubs were spending money and we didn't want to spend hundreds and thousands of pounds and still be in the same boat at the end of the season. Yes, we could have invested more. I'm not saying we had lots more but we could have bought in players. Richard Webster was coming here but Bath doubled their offer and we couldn't compete. It got to the stage when we couldn't compete in the money stakes and in the professional era it is all down to money. A lot of people are investing now and just as the Coventrys and Southamptons of this world will always find money, the Manchester Uniteds and Liverpools will raise more.

'Frano Botica was to have been our linchpin. He had shown us what he was capable of and losing him was a big blow. We are still negotiating with our lawyers on the question of compensation for Botica. Llanelli still owe us money. But that was a sound financial deal on our part. And how can Llanelli, with debts of £500,000, buy him? We have always had strong Colts and junior teams here and more and more players are developing nicely. There are kids, though, who still want to make their name at Central Park, but we have had to compete with the top international players in the country, the Jeremy Guscotts of this world, and we don't want to do that with players who don't quite make it in rugby league. I think the lads like Gary Connolly who had a spell in union found how difficult a game it can be. Rugby league still takes players and we have to work very, very hard to keep them. This is not a sad day. It is the start of a new era. I don't want people to be sorry for us. I know there is a lot of goodwill out there and I appreciate that, but we don't want people's pity. We want their respect, and I feel we have achieved a tremendous amount to be proud about over the last ten years.

'Since Super League started we felt many Wigan followers would watch us. That has not been the case. They haven't deemed to come out of their bunker. The problem has then been a bit of a spiral. Players leave you, the crowd is down, sponsors don't come and bar takings are down. But we live in hope. And I'm not cynical. We want to keep players and have had to revamp the structure. We hope our new wage bill will be fair to players but we'll work within our budget. All right, professionalism doesn't rest easy on my shoulders. I'm one of the old school. But professionalism won't go away and now we have this mish-mash.'

And it is a mish-mash. The longer you stay with Orrell, the more the professional game seems to be a mish-mash of contradictions. The day before the match, 'Des's Army' have been battling away again. On Friday mornings a group of members are hard at it, painting the corner of the terrace, all volunteers like past president Bob Gaskell, all part of an invisible workforce of unpaid helpers on whom the game has depended for a century. And as Saracens' team coach arrives from north London and out clambers François Pienaar, for whom this must seem a world away from Ellis Park, in one of the Edge Hall Road bars Charlie Cusani pours a member a drink. Cusani is a bar steward and he's playing in Orrell's second row that afternoon. Pienaar earns more than this Orrell team put together, and when you're on £8,000, for Cusani every little helps.

The Under-15 side receives its three trophies and has a team picture taken in the pouring rain. 'Try to smile, Des,' someone shouts. And still it pours down. Someone is gamely trying to keep a barbecue alight in the rain and from the back of a car a whole lamb is being raffled. In the tiny stand sits Nigel Wray, the man whose money has bought Pienaar and the expensively acquired Saracens team. As the rain blows into the stand and around 800 people huddle together to generate some warmth – and this is the last weekend in April, for goodness sake – you feel some sympathy for Wray's view that facilities at grounds are in-adequate and perhaps we need a little pampering. The match has an end-of-season feel, with Saracens, middle of the table and with nothing much to play for, running out winners by 44–22. Orrell's wretched luck is summed up when Alex Bennett storms away and throws a pass which is intercepted by Richard Hill on the halfway line. The Lions flanker runs half the length of the pitch to score Saracens' third try just before the break. The refereeing is as dreadful as the weather and only two late tries by Matthew McCarthy and Stuart Turner help reflect the play and end Orrell's last home game in the top division on a high note. Nigel Wray gives an interview to a radio reporter in which he says there will be 'casualties' in the new era, a group of Saracens supporters in red fezes give a muted cheer, and we all troop back to the welcoming warmth of the clubhouse.

In the car park, just at the moment Lawrence Dallaglio is receiving the Courage League trophy, one of Orrell's young forwards breaks down on the shoulder of a member of his family. 'I can't take much more of this, I really can't.' He is inconsolable. But there is a light in all this gloom. Next season Orrell are to receive £500,000 as part of the deal between the league's new sponsors Allied Dunbar and Sky television. A new director of rugby will come to Edge Hall Road and across town there could be a new salvation. David Whelan may not be handing over his shop profits to Orrell just yet, but he has offered them a lease on a new 28,000 all-seat stadium he wants to build in the Robin Park area of town. There are no strings attached, although Des Seabrook admits that the emotional attachment to Edge Hall Road may be difficult to break.

The evening before, Bolton Wanderers play their last game at Burnden Park in a very different atmosphere. They are to move to a new 25,000 all-seat stadium, Reebok Park, and are about to float on the stock exchange. And they are returning to the Premier League. Their club president Nat Lofthouse admits he is sad to go. 'But leaving Burnden Park does not necessarily mean losing all the great memories.' Derby and Sunderland, too, have plans to leave stadiums that are resonant more of the age of steam than the age of the Internet. Perhaps Orrell, too, should cut the umbilical cord.

In the town the grand Victorian buildings of Market Place and Wallgate echo days past when Wigan was a prosperous centre of the Industrial Revolution. Orwell's Wigan pier is a museum now and there is a post-industrial feel to the town. The revolution in rugby union has put Orrell, the village team that dared take on the giants, into a temporary recession. I'll miss them.

Not everyone is as sentimental as me about Orrell, though. After one of their ritual defeats, a 62–5 trouncing by Wasps in March, the former England lock and now *Sunday Telegraph* rugby union correspondent Paul Ackford was scathing. Ackford, matey bloke though he is, nevertheless takes his critic's role seriously. Putting the verbal boot in, he wrote, 'When they go down, people will moan about the changing face of rugby, the loss of a once-great club, the destructive influences brought about by rich men and super-clubs. Some will even begin to suggest that next season's League One will be poorer for Orrell's absence. Rubbish. Orrell do not deserve top status because they are simply not good enough.'

There is no room for sentiment, then, in this brave new world. Ackford has a point, even if it is the kind of point the self-made Victorian industrialists of Wigan used to make, namely 'If I can drag myself up by the bootstraps, lad, so can anyone'. But Orrell are used to put-downs by snooty Quins. Famously, one Harlequins captain once described Orrell as 'a lay-by off the M6'. That description helped Orrell cock a snook to wealthier clubs over the years when, against all the odds, they did maintain their top status and Quins suffered all manner of defeats at Edge Hall Road. In 1996–97 Orrell were left stranded on the hard shoulder, but at least they avoided a financial crash.

CHAPTER SEVENTEEN

Rich-mond, Rich-mond

As the 1996–97 season passed into history, it was clear that in the top tier of the English game none of the clubs was standing still. I realised that when I made a routine call to Gloucester and they asked me if I had an e-mail address. A couple of weeks later, their derby match against Bristol found itself on the Internet. This was unfashionable old 'Glawster', for goodness sake, the homespun club scorning the new trend for spending money on foreign superstars. If he's good enough for Longlevens, he's good enough for us, and all that. Then Gloucester were given £2.5 million by the owner of the Arrows grand prix racing team, Tom Walkinshaw, who bought a 73 per cent stake in the club. From Damon Hill to Richard Hill. And Gloucester then announced that they were signing Philippe Saint-André, the French wing and captain, on a two-year contract, and Walkinshaw was flying to Bath in his helicopter to watch his new investment at the Rec.

If you had emerged, Rip-Van-Winkle-like, from some year-long slumber and woken up on 3 May 1997, you would have rubbed your eyes and like Victor Meldrew, just not have believed it. The political map of Britain had just turned red and club rugby in England was no longer recognisable. And the club least recognisable was Richmond. You remember them, they played at the Athletic Ground, had been founded in 1861 and hadn't really changed much since then. You could go along to Richmond at quarter to three on a Saturday afternoon and not really know the first team had a match. They shared their ground with London Scottish and the Barboured brigade at Richmond had rubbed shoulders with the *Prime of Miss Jean Brodie* brigade at London Scottish quite nicely for years. In the spring of 1996 Richmond were still in the Third Division. By 3 May 1997 they were in the Premier division of the new Allied Dunbar League and about to rub shoulders with Bath, Leicester and the computer nerds of Gloucester. Richmond now had status and money. They were very Rich-mond.

In April 1996 Richmond were taken over by Ashley Levett, a Monaco-based millionaire who had made his fortune on the copper markets. When Richmond won promotion to League Two that month it was with a group of young players who most onlookers thought would do well just to survive in the higher division. Then Ashley Levett's cheque-book came out and the squad was transformed. Ben Clarke, the England flanker, came from Bath to captain the side and a host of big names followed: Scott Quinnell from Wigan, his younger brother Craig from Llanelli, Andy Moore and Adrian Davies from Cardiff. Allan Bateman and Jim Fallon returned from spells in rugby league and Simon Mason, the new Ireland full-back, joined from Orrell. On and off the field the club was transformed. Levett and his chief executive Symon Elliott began a five-year plan to turn the club into a profit-making concern. The players soon gelled and eventually won the Second Division title under the tutelage of their gruff coach John Kingston. Match-days were marketed in a brash, over-the-top way, with rock music waking half of Kew and goose-pimpled dancers gyrating on the pitch. Rob Orbison's 'It's Over' would herald each successful penalty and conversion. And there were plenty of those, as Richmond ran up 986 points and only lost one league game.

'But it's not a rugby club,' people moaned. And it's not any longer. Levett's aim is to create an all-purpose sports and entertainments group which he and Elliott have dubbed 'the Richmond Experience'. At the end of the season Richmond took over the basketball team Richmond Jaguars, who had been languishing in the Third Division of the National League and play pretty much unnoticed at Brunel University. Richmond also have plans to add an ice-hockey team and possibly to organise a ground-share with a rugby league club in an entire west London sporting empire along the lines of that envisaged by Sir John Hall in Newcastle. 'Our aim is to create a family of Richmond-branded teams but we're not interested in soccer, which is too mature a sport,' said Levett. 'The big question facing us now is whether rugby union by itself is enough. The way forward is to create multi-sports clubs using the same training and fitness facilities, the same colours, brand and ground.'

'We call it "the Richmond Experience",' said Elliott, 'and it's based on three elements that make up the Richmond brand: heritage, quality and innovation.' Elliott speaks in a language unfamiliar to most people's ears. He talks of the club's 'infra-structure' and of young players as 'feedstock'. All this doesn't go down too well with the conservative rugby stalwart, but the brand, sorry, the team played some excellent rugby during the season, albeit with a group of players taught and nurtured at other clubs. 'Money is no guarantee of success. If it were, Manchester United would have won the title for the last 20 years,' says John Kingston. True. But what Richmond have to ensure is that they don't end up as rugby union's Blackburn Rovers, a side bought through the largesse of their owner Jack Walker who were champions one minute and the 17th best side in the Premiership the next.

Richmond's spending continued with the arrival in the summer of the Argentinian scrum-half Agustin Pichot and his compatriot, the flanker Rolando Martin. By the end of the season Richmond could field a team of internationals. But even they realised that they had to put down roots. An Academy has been set up to attract young talent to the club which already has a thriving mini and youth rugby section. The Academy will develop players from 18 and upwards and two of its players, Andrew Beattie and Ben Leigh, have forced their way into the first team. Richmond have already begun scouting the country for talent, with Lee Best, a wing from Durham School and a member of the England Schools

Grand Slam-winning side, opting to join them. Richmond have also forged links with rugby-playing schools Llandovery and Bryanston. Richmond are, perhaps, the most nakedly commercial rugby set-up in the country. They have a business rather than a rugby mentality and the idea of a sporting empire does sound vainglorious in the eyes of rugby people, but the club realises that it has to produce and not just buy in talent.

Richmond may not be everybody's cup of tea. At the end of the 1996–97 season they held a rather self-congratulatory press conference at the Hard Rock Café opposite London's Green Park. The club produced a glossy brochure outlining its strategies and documenting its successes during the season. We all stood around a bit self-consciously, eating corn chips and guacamole while videos played endless reruns of Richmond games and the players in their club leisurewear sipped mineral water. 'I'm too much of an old curmudgeon for all this. I'm off,' said one of the more seasoned reporters. But you need, in the horrible new argot of the day, a new mind-set to watch Richmond. After 12 months, only the red, black and yellow jerseys are the same.

Ironically, one of the oldest clubs in the land has shaken up the cosy order at the top of the game. And another irony. Among the well-paid stars, Richmond's first team usually found room for an amateur player, an old gent of the old school. Brian Moore was happy to play for nothing but a £200 win bonus. At the end of the season he retired from the first-class game and the fanfare was so loud you could hear it in, well, Richmond High Street. 'The amount of coverage he's had in the national press could be recorded on the back of a postage stamp,' said Ashley Levett. And this was the same Brian Moore who for years had locked horns with the mandarins of Twickenham, demanding that international players be rewarded. Who knows what he's started?

CHAPTER EIGHTEEN

The Cotton Club

The five-paragraph story in *The Guardian* of 7 May 1974 was squeezed in between a report of World Team Tennis and news that Ken Buchanan would be defending his world lightweight title that month. The 200 words were blunt and matter-of-fact. 'The Lions left Heathrow Airport last night at the start of their 22-match tour of South Africa. The tour opens against Western Transvaal on 15 May and ends with the fourth Test against South Africa at Johannesburg on 27 July,' it began. There was a photograph of the tour captain Willie John McBride, Bobby Windsor and Gareth Edwards smiling as they walked through customs. There was no television coverage of the departure, no 12-page colour supplements in the newspapers and there had been little of the endless speculation of who was to tour in glossy rugby magazines.

In fact, the blandness of that report ignored the fact that this tour had run foul of the Labour government of the day which objected to it because of South Africa's apartheid policies, and its writer could never have guessed at how successful McBride's team were to be in the Republic. Low-key though the send-off was, the 1974 Lions returned to be heralded as perhaps the greatest to have left these shores. The Lions won three of the four

Tests and drew the fourth, the first time South Africa had lost a full-scale series at home this century. There is a memorable photograph that really does say more than a thousand words. J.J. Williams, the Llanelli wing, is scoring a try in one of the Tests at Port Elizabeth and the black faces penned in behind the razor-wire are smiling broadly.

'Rugby union was a relatively minor sport here then, but in South Africa the interest was phenomenal,' says David Frost, who covered the tour for *The Guardian.* 'There were a dozen or so reporters on tour and I used to telex reports and had little or no contact with the sports desk. Rugby writing then was more serious; there was more analysis of the play and, because of the lack of television coverage, more descriptive writing. The players were great fun to be with, but it has to be said that there was a certain amount of, what shall we call it, high jinks on that tour. I can't see touring players being given that amount of licence nowadays.'

One of the tourists in 1974 was the Yorkshire schoolteacher Ian McGeechan, who remembers the Lions players receiving 25 pence a day expenses. McGeechan was given time off to tour by an indulgent head teacher. 'We met up in London for two days and had one training session,' he recalls. 'It was a lot more low-key in those days but because we had about eight weeks before the first Test in South Africa we could concentrate on our preparation once we'd flown out there. The Test matches used to be broadcast on the radio here and highlights shown on television about a week later. It was less of a media event, everything was more personal and we all felt a long way from home. In 1974 everything was at a distance.'

McGeechan is talking in the boardroom of Sky television in the west London suburb of Isleworth. The 1997 Lions tour management, a group of players and a group of journalists are all nibbling on king prawns and pieces of chicken which are washed down with bottles of Lion lager. The sun is slanting through the windows. Close your eyes and this could be a barbecue on a lawn in Pretoria or Bloemfontein, two of the venues for the trip of 13 matches which is being billed as 'the First Professional Lions Tour' or, for the really vulgar, 'the £1 Million Lions Tour'.

The 50-year-old McGeechan, director of rugby at Northampton, is the tour coach. It is his third trip in this role following tours to Australia and New Zealand in 1989 and 1993. When David Frost and his colleagues were covering the 1974 tour they would be given a piece of paper at the East India Club with the names of the tourists and would write what they liked. In the Sky boardroom in 1997 there are as many journalists as had been at Conservative Central Office that morning to receive copies of the Tory's election manifesto. Everywhere you looked, someone – McGeechan, the Lions manager Fran Cotton, the tour committee chairman Ray Williams and players Keith Wood, Jason Leonard and Robert Howley – was being interviewed.

There is a satellite link-up to Johannesburg, where the former Springbok fly-half Naas Botha gives his views on the Lions selection. Naas is surprised that Nick Popplewell, 'the younger Quinnell' and someone he refers to as 'Michael Catt' aren't touring. There is also a link-up to Leicester where the Tigers' six new Lion cubs, including the new captain Martin Johnson, take it in turns to say how 'delighted' they are to be touring. One ritual that hasn't changed is that the players received their letters of invitation in the post that morning. Poor old Jonathan Davies, who had been interviewed on Radio Four at 8.30 a.m., clearly hadn't bumped into his postman because he was still hoping for an invite. But if Davies had read his *Daily Mail* that day he would have known the worst. Curiously, the *Mail*'s newshound Peter Jackson has already named the squad – and in 34 out of 35 cases he is right.

Far from being paid 25 pence a day and having to cadge money for phone calls home from the likes of David Frost, these 35 Lions are being paid a flat fee of £12,000 with appearance money on top. The insurance firm Scottish Provident put £400,000 directly into underpinning the tour and another £350,000 into promotion. The company's logo is plastered across the shirts. Virgin Atlantic are the tour's official airline.

The day after the Sky press conference, newspapers devote acres of space to the tour selections. The 1997 Lions include 18 Englishmen, eight Welshmen, five Scots and four Irishmen, a fair reflection of the season's Five Nations Championship. There is the predictable outraged reaction from the Celtic papers on the snubs to certain of their players and Davies, in particular, would have been the sentimental choice of most rugby followers. But the parochial reaction is not confined to Welsh, Scottish and Irish papers. Searching for its local angle, the back-page headline in London's *Evening Standard* roared: 'Lions Snub for London. Only five chosen from capital's four top clubs.' It went on to list the snubbed. Well, there was that well-known Cockney Kyran Bracken . . . and there was, er, Kyran Bracken . . .

But whatever the selections, the first professional Lions left Heathrow on 17 May as the best prepared and most meticulously chosen in history. Since the previous October, Ian McGeechan had spent hours sitting in dark rooms at the Centre for Notational Analysis in Cardiff where he had scrutinised the individual Lions candidates. 'With digitally marked tape I've been able to see a player perform in various elements of the game,' said McGeechan. 'And I have been able to target players or certain phases of the game. I can go to the computer to see how many tackles, say, Scott Gibbs makes in a match, or how many tackles are made from a ruck. The videos have been invaluable.'

Cotton is the perfect foil to the cerebral McGeechan. Another member of the 1974 tour, the former England prop had been unusually restless during the season. This was understandable, as in 1982 Cotton was banned by the Rugby Football Union for ten years for writing a book. Now he was making up for lost time. In 1996–97 Cotton not only became the voice of the Lions management, he also became the booming voice of the grass-roots of the game in the struggle for power with the owner clubs, forming an unlikely alliance with Cliff Brittle, the chairman of the RFU committee.

Instead of sulking during his ban, Cotton set up the leisure-wear firm Cotton Traders with his former Sale and England team-mate Steve Smith. During the season the Altrincham-based firm sold the rights to produce the England shirt to Reebok for around £2 million.

However well prepared the Lions were, though, and however many commercial spin-offs the tour provided, can the Lions continue into the next century in the professional era? After all, the clubs have their players under contract and Sir John Hall, for one, was incredulous during the week of the Lions selection that five of his players would be deprived of their well-earned rest during the summer. Ray Williams insisted that the show would go on. 'The unions concerned have all reaffirmed their support for tours until the year 2011. Now the markers for international rugby are the World Cups and Lions tours. The Lions tours will feature strongly in the international programme during the next century,' he said.

There was a missionary aspect to the early Lions tours, a sense that the best of the British were out there not just to teach the Southern Hemisphere how to play the game but to teach them the spirit of the game too. No such well-meaning illusions existed in 1997 when Fran Cotton chose a Lions squad very much in his own image, with hard, unyielding and unsmiling forwards epitomised by the selection of the mean-looking Johnson as captain. Cotton was well aware that there was a paucity of match-winning three-quarters in 1974. The success of that tour was forged primarily on the anvil of forward power.

And so the Lions departed, a weary bunch after the first hectic and bruising season of professional rugby in Britain. The tour was arguably the most talked-about sporting event in Britain during the year but, as in 1974, the majority of rugby supporters back home were deprived of the moving pictures. On the day before the 1995 World Cup final in South Africa, Rupert Murdoch bought up the rights to show all rugby in the Southern Hemisphere, including Lions tours. And so there we were at the headquarters of Sky. Without our dishes, though, we were deprived of the rugby feast we had savoured all season.